CAMPAIGN • 236

OPERATION *POINTBLANK* 1944

Defeating the Luftwaffe

STEVEN J ZALOGA

Series editor Marcus Cowper

First published in 2011 by Osprey Publishing
Midland House, West Way, Botley, Oxford OX2 0PH, UK
44-02 23rd St, Suite 219, Long Island City, NY 11101, USA

E-mail: info@ospreypublishing.com

A CIP catalog record for this book is available from the British Library.

ISBN: 978 1 84908 385 0

E-book ISBN: 978 1 84908 386 7

Editorial by Ilios Publishing Ltd, Oxford, UK (www.iliospublishing.com)
Page layout by: The Black Spot
Index by Marie-Pierre Evans
Typeset in Sabon and Myriad Pro
Maps by Bounford.com
3D bird's-eye views by The Black Spot
Battlescene illustrations by Steven J. Zaloga
Originated by PDQ Media
Printed in China through Worldprint

10 11 12 13 14   10 9 8 7 6 5 4 3 2 1

www.ospreypublishing.com

AUTHOR'S NOTE

The standard abbreviation for Luftwaffe units identifies the *Gruppen* within a *Geschwader* by Roman numerals, and the *Staffeln* by Arabic numerals. So II/Jagdgeschwader 1 was II Gruppe, Jagdgeschwader 1; and 2./Jagdgeschwader 1 was Staffel 2, Jagdgeschwader 1.

COVER IMAGE CREDIT

NARA.

THE WOODLAND TRUST

Osprey Publishing are supporting the Woodland Trust, the UK's leading woodland conservation charity, by funding the dedication of trees.

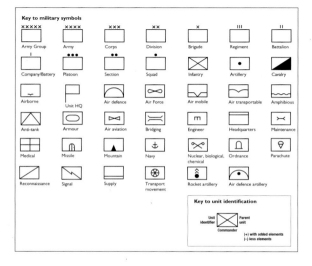

CONTENTS

INTRODUCTION

Operation *Pointblank* was among the most decisive air campaigns of World War II. Initiated in the summer of 1943, it aimed to cripple the German fighter force in advance of Operation *Overlord* – the amphibious invasion of Normandy in 1944. Although the campaign ostensibly was part of the Combined Bomber Offensive by both the Royal Air Force (RAF) and the US Army Air Force (USAAF), in practice, the mission was undertaken primarily by the USAAF. The USAAF's conduct of the campaign is the focus of this book.

The initial stage of the campaign revealed serious flaws in USAAF doctrine, especially its reliance on "self-defending" heavy bombers to conduct daytime precision-bombing missions. Raids against the ball-bearing industry around Schweinfurt in the summer and autumn of 1943 proved unexpectedly costly, and delayed the start of the final phase of the campaign. The solution was the use of long-range escort fighters such as the P-47D Thunderbolt and P-51B Mustang. The Luftwaffe remained convinced through the end of 1943 that improvements in fighter weapons and tactics would continue to cause such severe attrition against the USAAF daytime bombers that the campaign would be defeated. By early 1944 the USAAF had accumulated sufficient heavy bombers and escort fighters to initiate the final phase of Operation *Pointblank*, codenamed *Argument*. In the final week of February 1944 the Eighth Air Force launched systematic bombing attacks on the German aircraft industry, while at the same time staging a broader campaign against German day fighters by means of more aggressive fighter tactics. This "Big Week" did not defeat the Luftwaffe, but it marked a major turning point in the air campaign. German losses, especially the loss of experienced fighter pilots, were so debilitating that the Luftwaffe never fully recovered. The relentless campaign in the spring of 1944 continued to batter the Luftwaffe fighter force and won daytime air superiority over Germany for the USAAF. By the time of the Normandy landings on D-Day in June 1944, the Luftwaffe fighter force had been decisively defeated and thereafter failed to present a significant barrier to Allied operations in northwest Europe.

OPPOSITE
In late May through most of June 1944, the Eighth Air Force was diverted to missions over France to support the Operation *Overlord* invasion. Here, a weathered B-17 of the 100th Bombardment Group bombs coastal defenses near Boulogne on June 5, 1944, the day before D-Day. (NARA)

Defense of the Reich, mid-February 1944

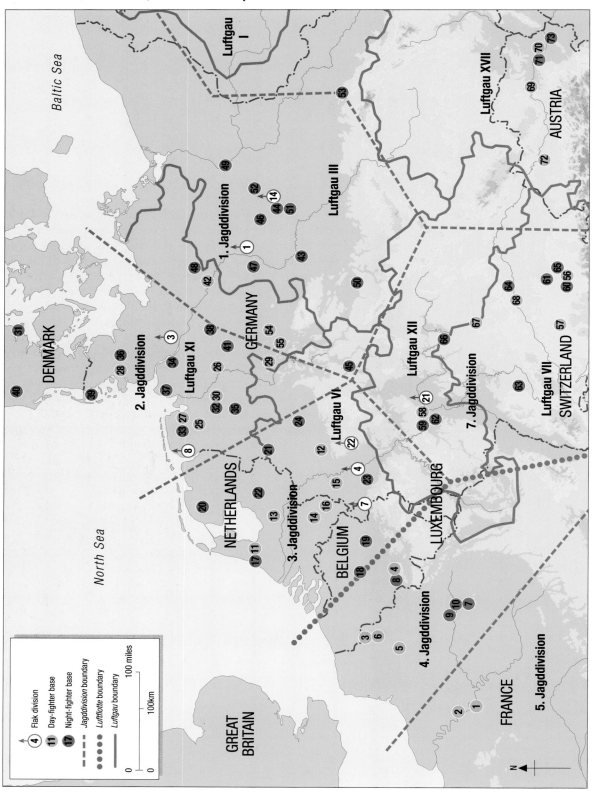

MAP #	AIRBASE	UNIT	MAP #	AIRBASE	UNIT
		Luftflotte 3	36	Schleswig	II Nachtjagdgeschwader 3
		5. Jagddivision	37	Nordholz	7/Nachtjagdgeschwader 3
1	Cormelles	Stab Jagdgeschwader 2, III/Jagdgeschwader 2	38	Lüneberg	8/Nachtjagdgeschwader 3
2	Creil	II/Jagdgeschwader 2	39	Westerland	IV/Nachtjagdgeschwader 3
		4. Jagddivision	40	Grove	10/Nachtjagdgeschwader 3
3	Lille-Nord	Stab Jagdgeschwader 26, 4/Jagdgeschwader 26	41	Fassberg	II/Nachtjagdgeschwader 4
4	Florennes	I/Jagdgeschwader 26			1. Jagddivision
5	Grévillers	5/Jagdgeschwader 26, 7/Jagdgeschwader 26	42	Ludwigslust	III/Jagdgeschwader 54; II/Jagdgeschwader 302
6	Vendeville	III/Jagdgeschwader 26	43	Zerbst	III/Jagdgeschwader 301
7	Chenay	Stab/Nachtjagdgeschwader 4	44	Jüterborg	I/Jagdgeschwader 302
8	Florennes	I/Nachtjagdgeschwader 4	45	Kassel	I/Nachtjagdgeschwader 2
9	Athies-sous Laon	2/Nachtjagdgeschwader 4	46	Döberitz	Stab Nachtjagdgeschwader 5; Stab
10	Juvincourt	III/Nachtjagdgeschwader 4			Jagdgeschwader 302
			47	Stendal	I/Nachtjagdgeschwader 5
		Luftflotte Reich	48	Parchim	II/Nachtjagdgeschwader 5
		3. Jagddivision	49	Königsberg	III/Nachtjagdgeschwader 5
11	Amsterdam	Stab JG1	50	Erfurt	IV/Nachtjagdgeschwader 5
12	Dortmund	I/Jagdgeschwader 1, Sturm/Jagdgeschwader 1	51	Brandis	9/Nachtjagdgeschwader 5
13	Zeist	II/Jagdgeschwader 1	52	Werneuchen	Nachtjagdgeschwader 10 IA
14	Volkel	III/Jagdgeschwader 1	53	Luben	4/Nachtjagdgeschwader 200
15	München-Gladbach	I/Jagdgeschwader 3	54	Völkenrode	I/Zerstörergeschwader 26
16	Venlo	IV/Jagdgeschwader 3	55	Hildesheim	II/Zerstörergeschwader 26
17	Amsterdam	Stab Nachtjagdgeschwader 1, Stab			7. Jagddivision
		Nachtjagdgeschwader 2,	56	Neubiberg	Stab/Jagdgeschwader 3;
		II/Nachtjagdgeschwader 2, Stab Jagdgeschwader			II/Zerstörergeschwader 76
		300	57	Wörishofen	III/Jagdgeschwader 3
18	Brussels	I/Nachtjagdgeschwader 1	58	Wiesbaden	II/Jagdgeschwader 27
19	St Trond	II/Nachtjagdgeschwader 1	59	Wiesbaden	III/ Jagdgeschwader 300
20	Leeuwarden	IV/Nachtjagdgeschwader 1	60	Neubiberg	I/Jagdgeschwader 301
21	Rheine	10/Nachtjagdgeschwader 1	61	Schleissheim	Stab/Nachtjagdgeschwader 6;
22	Twente	III/Nachtjagdgeschwader 2			II/Nachtjagdgeschwader 6;
23	Bonn-Hangelar	I/Jagdgeschwader 300			Stab/Jagdgeschwader 301
24	Münster	II/Jagdgeschwader 300; I/Nachtjagdgeschwader 7	62	Mainz-Finthen	I/Nachtjagdgeschwader 6
		2. Jagddivision	63	Stuttgart	5/Nachtjagdgeschwader 6;
25	Zwischenahn	20/Jagdgeschwader 1			II/Nachtjagdgeschwader 102
26	Rotenburg	II Jagdgeschwader 3	64	Ingolstadt	Stab Nachtjagdgeschwader 101;
27	Jever	Stab Jagdgeschwader 11			I/Nachtjagdgeschwader 101
28	Husum	I/Jagdgeschwader 11	65	Munich-Riem	II/Nachtjagdgeschwader 101
29	Wunstorf	II/Jagdgeschwader 11; Stab Zerstörergeschwader 26;	66	Kitzingen	Stab Nachtjagdgeschwader 102;
		III/Zerstörergeschwader 26			I/Nachtjagdgeschwader 102
30	Oldenburg	III/Jagdgeschwader 11	67	Ansbach	Stab Zerstörergeschwader 76;
31	Aalborg	10/Jagdgeschwader 11			I/Zerstörergeschwader 76
32	Oldenburg	III/Jagdgeschwader 302	68	Öttingen	III/Zerstörergeschwader 76 Austria
33	Wittmundhafen	III/ Nachtjagdgeschwader 1;	69	Fels-am-Wagram	I/Jagdgeschwader 27
		2/Nachtjagdgeschwader 2	70	Seyring	II/Jagdgeschwader 53
34	Stade	Stab Nachtjagdgeschwader 3;	71	Seyring	II/ Jagdgeschwader 301
		III/Nachtjagdgeschwader 3	72	Wels	II/Zerstörergeschwader 1
35	Vechta	I/Nachtjagdgeschwader 3	73	Parndorf	II/Nachtjagdgeschwader 101

CHRONOLOGY

1942

August 17   First Eighth Air Force bomber mission to Rouen.

1943

April 5   First Eighth Air Force mission against a German aircraft plant at Antwerp, Belgium.

April 17   First Eighth Air Force mission against an aircraft plant in Germany, at Bremen.

May 21   First large-scale use of the WGr. 42 21cm rocket against bombers.

June 10   Plan for Combined Bomber Offensive formally released, initiating Operation *Pointblank*.

August 17   Mission against Schweinfurt incurs heavy casualties.

October 14   Second mission against Schweinfurt is so costly that further deep attacks into Germany are postponed for months.

October   First P-38 group deployed to VIII Fighter Command for escort duties.

December 5   First P-51B squadrons become operational in escort role.

1944

January 11   Mission to Oschersleben disrupted by weather and suffers heavy casualties, delaying Operation *Argument* another month.

January 24   First mission with escort fighters using aggressive new tactics authorized by Doolittle directive.

February 5   Luftwaffenbefelshaber Mitte becomes Luftflotte Reich.

February 20   Operation *Argument*, later called "Big Week," begins.

February 25   Big Week ends because of poor weather on February 26.

March 4   First Eighth Air Force mission to Berlin disrupted by weather.

March 6   First major US bomber attacks in the Berlin area.

April 1   Operation *Pointblank* formally ends, though missions continue.

April 20   Eisenhower's headquarters authorizes strikes against German synthetic-fuel plants.

May 12   Start of the "oil campaign" against synthetic-fuel plants.

June 6   Operation *Overlord* landings take place in Normandy.

THE STRATEGIC SETTING

The USAAF's Eighth Air Force began daytime heavy-bomber operations from England on August 17, 1942, with a raid by 12 B-17 bombers against Rouen, France. The scale of American bomber attacks in 1942 was small and experimental until the force could be built up enough to confront more stiffly defended targets deeper into Europe. Through the end of 1942 its operational strength averaged only about 100 bombers, and it was assigned only a single US fighter group for escort. Its build-up was slowed by the need to divert aircraft and personnel to the Twelfth Air Force to conduct combat operations in North Africa and Italy. The focus of the bomber attacks in early 1943 was the German submarine force, including submarine bases at Lorient and St Nazaire as well as submarine yards on Germany's North Sea coast such as at Bremen and Wilhelmshaven. By April 1943 the Eighth Air Force had only 264 heavy bombers and 172 escort fighters in England. The first mission against a German aircraft factory was conducted on April 5, 1943, against the Erla plant in Antwerp in Belgium and the first mission against an aircraft factory in Germany itself was conducted on April 17, 1943, against the Fw-190 plant in Bremen.

B-24D Liberators of the 2nd Bombardment Wing attack shipyards in the Dunkirk area on February 15, 1943. French harbors and German targets along the North Sea coast were the most common targets in the first Eighth Air Force missions. (NARA)

Escort-fighter ranges

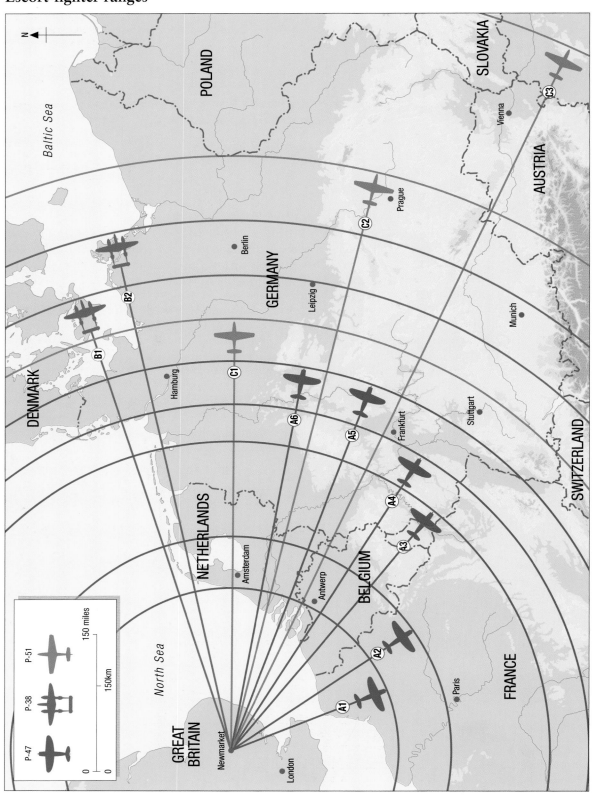

The Eighth Air Force in 1943 suffered a frequent dilution of strength because of frequent transfer of its bomber squadrons to the Mediterranean theater to support operations in North Africa, Sicily, and Italy. "Jerk's Natural," a B-24D-1 of the 93rd Bombardment Group is seen here in England in 1943 after having returned from Mediterranean missions. It was lost over Austria on October 1, 1943. (NARA)

The short-range bomber missions from the autumn of 1942 through the spring of 1943 could be only partly protected by USAAF and RAF fighter escorts, which lacked the range of the heavy bombers. Missions into Germany could be escorted part of the way to the target area, and then during the return leg of the trip. Although losses during this initial period were sometimes costly, they were not heavy enough to cause US commanders to doubt the core idea of USAAF tactical doctrine: the viability of the self-defending bomber in daytime precision bombing. Losses in 1942 averaged 4.5 percent per mission, climbing to 7.1 percent in the first quarter of 1943 and 7.6 percent in the second quarter. Grossly exaggerated kill claims by the bombers' gunners led to the mistaken belief that the attacks were causing severe losses to the German fighter force.

	Range (miles)	With drop tanks	Date
P-47			
A1	175	none (P-47C)	May 1943
A2	230	none (P-47D)	June 1943
A3	340	75-gallon belly	July 1943
A4	375	108-gallon belly	August 1943
A5	425	150-gallon belly	February 1944
A6	475	2 x 108-gallon wing	February 1944
P-38			
B1	520	none	November 1943
B2	585	2 x 108-gallon wing	February 1944
P-51			
C1	475	none	January 1944
C2	650	2 x 75-gallon wing	March 1944
C3	850	2 x 108-gallon wing	March 1944

B-17F heavy bombers of 324th Squadron, 91st Bombardment Group, head out from their base at Bassingbourne to targets toward Rouen on March 17, 1943. The bomber in the center of this photo is the best-known aircraft of the early campaign, "Memphis Belle." Piloted by Captain Robert Morgan, its crew was the first in the Eighth Air Force to survive their 25-mission tour, on May 17, 1943. (NARA)

RIGHT
A core element of USAAF doctrine was the belief that heavy bombers had adequate defensive armament to fend off fighter attacks during daytime missions. This is the waist position of a B-17 showing Staff Sergeant Robert L. Taylor manning the .50-cal heavy machine gun. He is wearing electrically heated gloves and boots for high-altitude operations as well as a flak apron. (NARA)

As the pace of USAAF daytime attacks began to expand, the Luftwaffe responded by increasing the size of its day-fighter force. Much of the defense against the early USAAF bomber strikes came from forward-deployed fighter units of Luftflotte 3 (Air Fleet 3) in France and fighter units based in the Netherlands. The Luftwaffe's heavy combat losses in the spring and summer of 1943 on the Russian and Mediterranean fronts made it difficult to form enough new fighter units, and much of the increase in Luftwaffe fighter strength in Germany came at the expense of the other theaters, with fighter units being drawn back into the Reich to deal with the American threat. The Luftwaffe day-fighter force for Reich defense continued to grow through 1943, though there was a spirited debate over whether day fighters, night fighters, or flak should receive priority.

In the summer of 1943 Allied leaders authorized the initiation of the Combined Bomber Offensive, also known as Operation *Pointblank*. In fact, the name papered over the fundamental disagreement between the RAF and USAAF over the conduct of the strategic-bombing campaign. Air Marshal Arthur Harris of RAF Bomber Command insisted that night area attacks on German cities would lead to a collapse of German civilian morale and destroy enough housing to seriously impact German industry. The USAAF was convinced that daytime precision bombing of German industry was a more effective approach. Operation *Pointblank* tried to reorient the focus of the strategic-bombing campaign toward the "intermediate" goal of defeating the Luftwaffe fighter force. The USAAF took up the *Pointblank* mission with enthusiasm since US doctrine considered the defeat of the Luftwaffe an essential prelude to a broader campaign against German war industries. The senior Allied army commanders wanted the Luftwaffe suppressed prior to the start of Operation *Overlord*, scheduled for the late spring of 1944, and so supported the *Pointblank* plan. Harris continued to insist on his indirect night-bombing approach, and so the burden of *Pointblank*'s initial goal against the Luftwaffe fell on the USAAF.

ABOVE
One of the iconic images of the air war over Germany was taken during Mission 104 to Emden on September 27, 1943. In the center is B-17F "Skippy" of the 570th Squadron, 390th Bombardment Group, which was later lost on a mission over France on February 5, 1944. Overhead are the contrails of P-47 fighters conducting their usual weaving maneuver to keep pace with the bombers. (NARA)

LEFT
A pair of B-17Fs of 322nd Squadron, 91st Bombardment Group, over England in 1943. The bomber in the foreground, "Mizpah/The Bearded Lady," was lost over Schweinfurt during the first raid on August 17, 1943. (NARA)

By the summer of 1943 the USAAF had become confident enough to begin missions into central Germany, even without fighter escort on the main leg of the mission. The prime targets were aircraft-assembly plants and the ball-bearing industry around Schweinfurt. Ball bearings had been selected for special attention since they were widely used in many military weapons,

DAY OF THE ROCKET GUNS: SCHWEINFURT, OCTOBER 14, 1943

By the autumn of 1943, the rocket-armed Bf-110 fighters of Zerstörergeschwader 26 and Zerstörergeschwader 76 had become one of the most effective tools to shatter the "Viermot Pulk," the B-17 combat box **(1)**. "Viermot" was the German pilots' nickname for the American heavy bombers, a slang contraction of the words for a four-engine bomber. The term "Pulk" means a throng in German but has long had a military meaning as a group; in the Slavic languages it means a regiment. The heavily armed Bf-110G-2/R3 seen here **(2)** was nicknamed the "Pulkzerstörer" ("Group Destroyer") for its intended mission of breaking up the bomber combat boxes. The Bf-110G-2/R-3 was armed with four launch tubes for the 21cm WGr. 42 **(3)** air-to-air rocket. Derived from the Army's 210mm Nebelwerfer artillery rocket, this projectile weighed 110kg (240lb) on launch and contained 10kg (22lb) of Amatol high explosive. Its time fuse was set to detonate at a predetermined range between 500–1,200m, and it also had an impact fuse in case of a direct hit. These weapons

were nicknamed "rocket guns" by American bomber crews, who were not aware of their actual configuration. Even if the spin-stabilized rockets were not especially accurate, the detonation of several of these weapons within a bomber box was usually sufficient to cause extensive fragmentation damage and to create enough chaos to cause the bombers to break formation. Once the bombers began to scatter, they would be attacked individually by the Bf-110G-2/R 2s using the 20mm MG 151 cannon **(4)** that were belly-mounted in a tray below the fuselage, which supplemented the two nose-mounted 30mm MK 108 cannon. On October 14 III/Zerstörergeschwader 26 departed its base at Wunstorf and headed south toward Schweinfurt, intercepting the bomber stream at around 1415hrs, around Wertheim. Of the 11 B-17 bombers claimed that day by the Geschwader, nine were claimed by fighters from this Gruppe. Zerstörergeschwader 76 claimed eight B-17 bombers that day, so the Bf 110 day fighters accounted for a quarter of the 74 B-17s claimed by I Jagdkorps.

including aircraft engines, and the German industry was geographically concentrated. Since the USAAF bomber force was still small, there was a special interest in finding these bottlenecks in German industry, an approach that Harris derided as "panacea targets." On August 17, 1943, the Eighth Air Force staged its largest and deepest-penetrating mission so far, a combined attack against the ball-bearing plants at Schweinfurt and the Bf-109 plant at Regensburg using 367 B-17 bombers. The force lost 60 bombers – 19 percent of those that reached the drop zone – which was an unsustainable rate of loss.

TOP
The northwest corner of Germany was the first region extensively hit by the Eighth Air Force in the second half of 1943. This is the attack on Bremen on October 8, 1943, by the 390th Bombardment Group, 3rd Bombardment Division. (NARA)

BOTTOM
A dramatic view of a bomber stream from 423rd Squadron, 306th Bombardment Group, heading for Bremen during one of the December 1943 missions. The aircraft in the lower-left foreground was interned in Switzerland on April 24, 1944. (NARA)

USAAF UNITS

1. 1st Bombardment Division
   (1st, 92nd, 303rd, 305th, 306th, 351st, 379th, 381st, and 384th Bombardment Groups)
1a 353rd Fighter Group
2. 3rd Bombardment Division
   (94th, 95th, 96th, 100th, 385th, 388th, and 390th Bombardment Groups)
2a 56th Fighter Group
3. 2nd Bombardment Division
   (93rd and 392rd Bombardment Groups)
3a 352nd Fighter Group

▼ **EVENTS**

1 Luftwaffe Seeräuber signals-intelligence station at Zeist reports first concentration of American bombers northeast of London at 1030hrs GMT. Fighter units in France, Netherlands, Belgium, Germany, and Denmark are alerted later in morning.

2 The 1st and 3rd Bombardment Divisions start to take off at 1012hrs; they depart the English coast around 1235hrs and the lead formations arrive over the Dutch coast around 1300hrs. Of 320 bombers dispatched, 229 carry out the mission. Fighter-escort penetration is shallow after running out of drop tanks; the 4th Fighter Group is unable to locate bombers and it returns to base; 78th and 355th Fighter Groups are ineffective because of autumn fog at bases. Only the 56th and 353rd Fighter Groups provide penetration escort.

3 The 2nd Bombardment Division departs the English coast around 1340hrs to stage a diversionary mission over the Channel, feinting an attack towards the northwestern German coast. Only 29 of 60 aircraft make formation because of the poor weather. Escort is provided by 352nd Fighter Group.

4 Fliegerkorps XII instructs units to avoid tangling with escorts, but III/Jagdgeschwader 1 and I/Jagdgeschwader 3 begin to engage with P-47s around Antwerp and lose seven fighters; 5/Jagdgeschwader 26 downs a 353th Fighter Group P-47 over Brugge, the first US fighter loss of the day.

5 The 1. Jagddivision fighter units are instructed to mass to the east of Aachen and strike the bomber stream after the P-47 escorts have left. However, some elements of Jagdgeschwader 26 begin attacking over Maastricht around 1330hrs.

6 The vast bulk of the 1. Jagddivision fighter units, especially Jagdgeschwader 1 and Jagdgeschwader 26, begin their attacks around 1340hrs in the Aachen area.

7 The 305th Bombardment Group flies off-course and north of the main bomber stream near Cologne, where it loses 13 of 16 bombers in a few minutes to massed German fighters of 1. Jagddivision.

8 The heavy fighters of Zerstörergeschwader 76 from the 7. Jagddivision, and Zerstörergeschwader 26 from the 2. Jagddivision, totaling 250 Bf-110s and 26 Me-410s, are directed into the bomber stream west of Schweinfurt. Zerstörergeschwader 76 starts rocket attacks against the 1st Bombardment Division near Limburg at around 1410hrs.

9 Zerstörergeschwader 26 begins rocket attacks against the 3rd Bombardment Division stream near Wertheim around 1430hrs.

10 German fighter attacks temporarily relent as the bombers reach their IP (initial point) on the approaches to Schweinfurt around 1430hrs, where the concentration of flak is heaviest.

11 Bombers conduct bomb runs on Schweinfurt from about 1435hrs to 1446hrs. Flak claims 42 bombers shot down.

12 Once the bombers emerge out of the flak concentrations, the fighters return, causing heavy losses. Fighter units from Jagdabschnittsführer Ostmark in Austria join the fray. Jagdgeschwader 27 has already hit the bomber stream west of Schweinfurt, and after 1500hrs it turns its attention to the returning bombers farther west over Nancy.

13 Jagdgeschwader 2 of Lufflotte 3 in France conducts a few sorties along the Dutch coast in the early afternoon, but saves its main effort for the late afternoon, when it hits the returning bomber stream from Verdun to Epernay from 1550 to 1700hrs, claiming ten more B-17 bombers.

14 The 1st and 3rd Bombardment Divisions begin to leave occupied Europe north of Dieppe around 1705hrs, and are back over England around 1725hrs. Bomber losses are 67, including one interned in Switzerland, and 138 damaged; German claims are 121 bombers. German fighter losses are around 48 fighters; US claims are 186 by the bombers, 13 by the fighters.

BLACK THURSDAY: THE SECOND SCHWEINFURT MISSION, OCTOBER 14, 1943

Deep attack into Germany without fighter escort again proves too costly for the USAAF

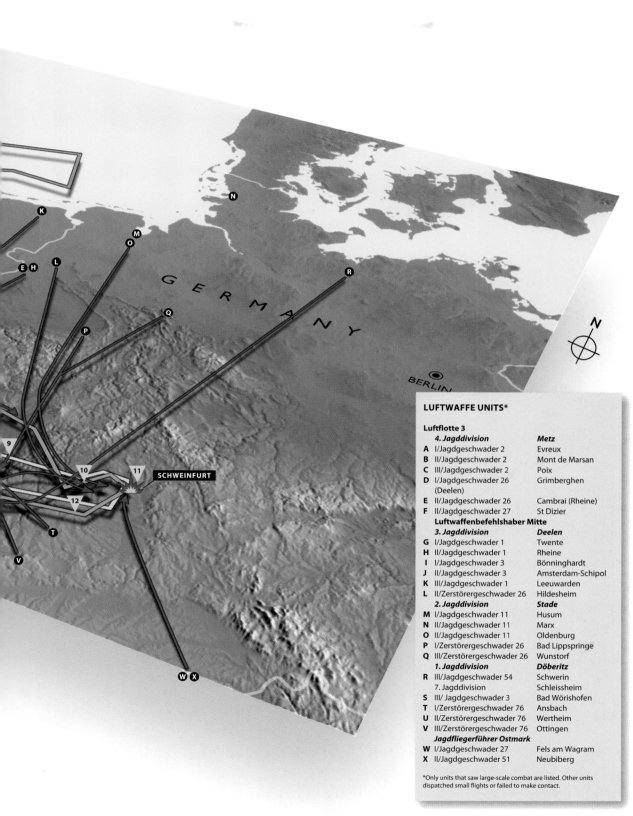

LUFTWAFFE UNITS*

Luftflotte 3

	4. Jagddivision	*Metz*
A	I/Jagdgeschwader 2	Evreux
B	II/Jagdgeschwader 2	Mont de Marsan
C	III/Jagdgeschwader 2	Poix
D	I/Jagdgeschwader 26 (Deelen)	Grimberghen
E	I/Jagdgeschwader 26	Cambrai (Rheine)
F	II/Jagdgeschwader 27	St Dizier

Luftwaffenbefehlshaber Mitte

	3. Jagddivision	*Deelen*
G	I/Jagdgeschwader 1	Twente
H	II/Jagdgeschwader 1	Rheine
I	I/Jagdgeschwader 3	Bönninghardt
J	II/Jagdgeschwader 3	Amsterdam-Schipol
K	III/Jagdgeschwader 1	Leeuwarden
L	II/Zerstörergeschwader 26	Hildesheim

	2. Jagddivision	*Stade*
M	I/Jagdgeschwader 11	Husum
N	II/Jagdgeschwader 11	Marx
O	II/Jagdgeschwader 11	Oldenburg
P	I/Zerstörergeschwader 26	Bad Lippspringe
Q	III/Zerstörergeschwader 26	Wunstorf

	1. Jagddivision	*Döberitz*
R	III/Jagdgeschwader 54	Schwerin
	7. Jagddivision	Schleissheim
S	III/ Jagdgeschwader 3	Bad Wörishofen
T	I/Zerstörergeschwader 76	Ansbach
U	II/Zerstörergeschwader 76	Wertheim
V	III/Zerstörergeschwader 76	Ottingen

	Jagdfliegerführer Ostmark	
W	I/Jagdgeschwader 27	Fels am Wagram
X	II/Jagdgeschwader 51	Neubiberg

*Only units that saw large-scale combat are listed. Other units dispatched small flights or failed to make contact.

RIGHT
The 21cm Bordrakete became one of the most effective supplements to fighter armament in late 1943 to deal with US heavy bombers. Single-engine fighters like this Fw 190A-4/R6 received two launch tubes. (NARA)

BOTTOM
An overhead view taken of the ball-bearing plants at Schweinfurt during the second raid on October 14, 1943. (NARA)

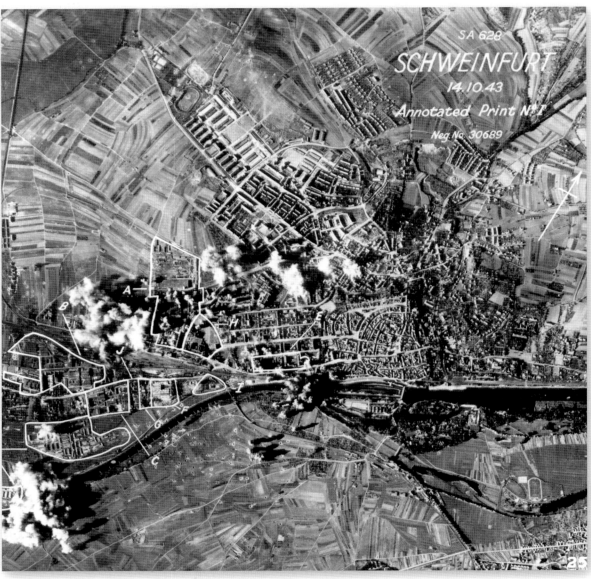

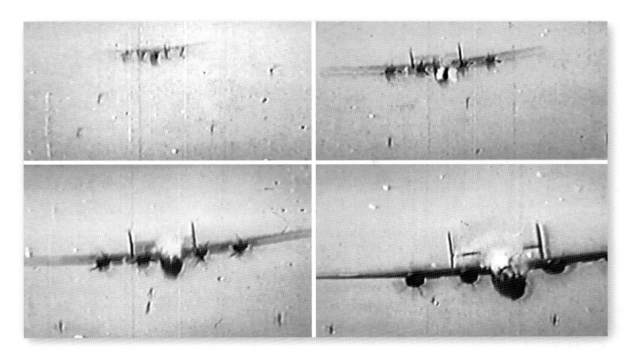

The Schweinfurt raid undermined USAAF faith in the viability of self-defending bombers. It was quite clear from operations research in 1943 that escort fighters substantially reduced the bombers' loss rate. Was it possible to develop a fighter with sufficient range to escort the bombers deep into Germany? In response to the Schweinfurt raid, the USAAF finally reoriented its policy on escort fighters and began accelerated efforts to develop long-range fighters for the Eighth Air Force. This requirement was approached from multiple angles, including the transfer of the long-range P-38 Lightning to the European Theater of Operations (ETO), the addition of more internal fuel tanks to the P-38 and P-47 fighters, and the development and production of drop tanks. In the long run, the most effective solution was the adoption of the new P-51 Mustang fighter. The process of creating a long-range escort-fighter force took several months, with drop tanks becoming available by the end of 1943 and the P-51 beginning to arrive in significant numbers by the beginning of 1944.

The Eighth Air Force campaign of autumn 1943 reached its climax on October 14, 1943, with a second mission against Schweinfurt. Of the 291 bombers taking part, 60 were lost, 17 suffered heavy damage, and 121 suffered reparable damage. The USAAF mistakenly believed that they had crippled German ball-bearing production, which was expected to have a cascading effect in disrupting the rest of German industry; in fact this did not occur. Regardless of the success of the mission, the loss rate was crippling. As a result, further deep-penetration missions into Germany were postponed until the long-range escort-fighter force could be built up. Besides the fighter reinforcements, the USAAF wanted a more substantial increase of the bomber force. The original plan envisioned the final phase of Operation *Pointblank* starting in November 1943, but this was postponed, at first because of delays in deploying escort fighters and more bombers. By the time the fighter and bomber strength had reached sufficient levels in January 1944, the winter weather over Germany again delayed plans.

Death of a B-24. This June 1944 gun-camera footage shows one of the dreaded "12 o'clock high" attacks from the perspective of an Fw-190A-7 pilot. The entire engagement seen here took only about a second. (Author's collection)

A Bf 110G-2/R-3 of Zerstörergeschwader 26 is readied for a mission. These rocket-armed heavy fighters proved very effective in the autumn 1943 campaign over western Germany. (NARA)

By the end of 1943 the Luftwaffe regarded the Reich defense mission as difficult but not hopeless. The Luftwaffe's primary nemesis was still the RAF, which accounted for about 175,000 tons of bombs dropped in 1943 compared with about 50,000 tons for the USAAF. The Luftwaffe's accelerated production program in combination with armament minister Albert Speer's industrial reforms led to a significant increase in fighter production at the start of 1944. The shock of novel British electronic-warfare tactics in the summer 1943 bombing campaign against the Ruhr industrial region had been addressed both by new tactics and technology, and the Luftwaffe was able to inflict savage losses on the British bomber force during its autumn and winter raids on Berlin in 1943–44. In combination with the heavy losses inflicted on US bombers over Schweinfurt, the Luftwaffe was hopeful that the strategic-bomber campaign had been stalemated and could be defeated in 1944. If the Luftwaffe assessment at the end of 1943 was cautiously optimistic, there were still some areas of concern. Pilot losses had been far higher than expected and experienced leaders were particularly hard hit; ten Knight's Cross recipients with combined victory tallies of over a thousand Allied aircraft had been killed during the 1943 campaign. Fuel shortages continued to constrain German pilot training, and the lack of trained pilots and mechanics limited the Luftwaffe's ability to build up new fighter units. Allied electronic countermeasures had substantially reduced the effectiveness of the Reich's heavy investment in flak batteries. Although Göring originally dismissed the threat of long-range escort fighters, by December 1943 it was becoming apparent that USAAF fighters might pose a greater threat.

OPPOSING COMMANDERS

LUFTWAFFE COMMANDERS

The most controversial figure in the Luftwaffe was its commander, **Reichsmarschall Hermann Göring**. Not only was Göring head of the Luftwaffe, he was also a key figure in Hitler's inner circle of Nazi loyalists, and earmarked as Hitler's successor. Göring had a distinguished career as a fighter pilot in the Great War, earning the Pour le Mérite (known informally as the "Blue Max") and commanding Jagdgeschwader Richthofen with 22 aerial victories to his credit. He was an early member of the Nazi Party, a genuine war hero, and one of Hitler's most famous and prominent supporters.

The senior Luftwaffe commanders on the terrace of the Luftwaffe headquarters in Berlin on July 6, 1941. From left to right: the Luftwaffe's chief of staff, Generaloberst Hans Jeschonnek, Reichsmarschall Hermann Göring, and Generaloberst Albert Kesselring, former chief of staff but at the time commander of Luftflotte 2. (Library of Congress)

Göring was a suave political operative and instrumental in negotiating Hitler's accession to power with President Hindenburg in 1933. After Hitler took power, Göring held a number of key government positions but he was most closely associated with the rebirth of the Luftwaffe. He became its commander-in-chief in 1935 and led the Luftwaffe through the war. Göring's political influence with Hitler in the late 1930s was vital to its meteoric growth. Air forces are extremely costly, and by 1940 Wehrmacht spending on weapons was divided roughly 6-to-3-to-1 with the Luftwaffe holding the favored position, followed by the Army and the Kriegsmarine (Navy). Göring was the archetypal Nazi empire builder, managing to absorb both the substantial flak force and the paratroops into his Luftwaffe.

Göring's fortunes waned with the decline of the Luftwaffe after 1942, and he became increasingly aloof from its day-to-day management. In contrast to Hitler's spartan lifestyle and workaholic schedule, Göring luxuriated in power, amassed a considerable fortune, and spent more and more time away from Berlin enjoying a decadent lifestyle. By 1943 he was no longer a favorite of Hitler's because of the Luftwaffe's frequent setbacks, and he attempted to compensate by blindly supporting Hitler's whims. He was widely scorned by Luftwaffe field commanders, nicknamed the "Rubber Lion." Göring's dysfunctional leadership style was later described by General der Flieger Karl Koller, the last Luftwaffe chief of staff:

> The Reichsmarschall delighted in playing one man off against the other, and it gave him malicious pleasure when the two protagonists were at each other's throats. He would stand nearby and make scornful comments to those around him. He often impressed me as being pleased with the disharmony reigning among his most important staff. It seemed that he had no interest in encouraging an atmosphere of smooth cooperation since he was afraid that this would create a united front against himself.

Göring's chief subordinate on the industrial side was **Generalfeldmarschall Erhard Milch**. Like Göring, Milch had served as a young airman in World War I. Unlike Göring, Milch stayed out of politics after the war and became director of Lufthansa in 1926. He earned Göring's gratitude by finding him a job after he had run afoul of state authorities for his political rabble rousing, and likewise Milch attracted Hitler's attention by providing air transport for Nazi leaders prior to their election victory in 1933. With the Nazi accession to power in 1933, Milch's political connections in combination with his administrative experience at Lufthansa led to his appointment as the head of the new German air ministry (Staatssekretär der Reichsluftfahrtministerium), the key position in the expansion of the German aviation industry. Milch's power was further extended in November 1941 when he took over as Luftwaffe *Generalluftzeugmeister* (air inspector general) following the suicide of Ernst Udet. This post was responsible for overseeing the technical development of German aircraft and so unified control over the aviation industry under Milch. Relations between Milch and Göring became increasingly strained as the war dragged on, with Milch joining the fighter faction along with fighter-advocate Adolf Galland, in opposition to Hitler, Göring, and Jeschonnek who favored bombers. Although Milch was instrumental in reorienting the industry toward fighter production in 1944, he was sacked in May 1944 after a violent argument with Hitler over the designation of the Me-262 jet as a fighter-bomber.

The Luftwaffe chief of staff and Milch's rival was **Generaloberst Hans Jeschonnek**. He served as a fighter pilot in 1918 but was ten years younger than Göring and Milch. Jeschonnek was an ardent Nazi who idolized Hitler; he enjoyed a meteoric rise from captain to general in five years from 1934 to 1939, becoming chief of staff in February 1939. He was eager, ambitious, and totally devoted to the Luftwaffe, but at the same time he was insecure and overbearing, showing little skill dealing with the many other powerful Luftwaffe commanders. Although he had served under Milch in the 1930s, they soon parted ways and grew deeply contemptuous of each other. Jeschonnek was instrumental in creating the archetypal 'blitzkrieg' air force with its emphasis on tactical-attack aircraft and dive-bombers, but he proved inflexible and shortsighted and did not see the need for a stronger fighter arm for Reich defense and neglected the heavy-bomber force. The Luftwaffe's failures in late 1942 and early 1943 led to Jeschonnek's growing isolation and depression, and after several failed attempts, he committed suicide in August 1943 following the RAF's devastating Peenemunde raid. He was replaced by **Generaloberst Günther Korten**, who had been an air fleet chief

The Luftwaffe fighter inspector Adolf Galland is seen here with Reichsmarschall Hermann Göring during a visit to Jagdgeschwader 26 "Schlageter," a fighter unit that was stationed in northwestern France and heavily involved in the early efforts against US daytime bomber attacks. (Library of Congress)

of staff in the 1939–40 campaign and commander of Luftflotte 1 in 1943. Korten was in this key position during one of its most challenging periods, and tried to reverse Jeschonnek's anti-fighter bias.

The initial Reich defense force, the Luftwaffenbefehlshaber Mitte (LBM: Luftwaffe Command Center), was headed by a flak officer, **Generaloberst Hubert Weise**, from its inception on March 24, 1941. The heavy destruction in the Ruhr caused by the RAF's summer bombing campaign led to a growing chorus of complaints to Hitler and Göring by the local Nazi Party *Gauleiters* (district leaders) about the completely inadequate performance of the Luftwaffe. As a result, there was a broad shakeup of Reich defense in the autumn of 1943, and the LBM was converted into the new Luftflotte Reich. Existing commanders, including Weise, were replaced by officers from other theaters not tainted by the previous failures. **Generaloberst Hans-Jürgen Stumpff** was the new Luftflotte Reich commander. Stumpff was Luftwaffe chief of staff until January 1939, when he was replaced by Jeschonnek. He subsequently served as commander of Luftflotte 1 in Prussia, and, after promotion to Generaloberst in May 1940, he served as commander of Luftflotte 5 in Norway until his November 1943 appointment to head Reich air defense.

The most prominent commander of the Reich fighter force in the early years of 1941–43 was **General der Flieger Josef Kammhuber**, who was commander of XII Fliegerkorps. This corps contained most of the Luftwaffe night-fighter force, so Kammhuber also served as the inspector of the night-fighter branch. Kammhuber started the war as commander of Kampfgeschwader 51 and his Ju-88 bomber was shot down during the French campaign in 1940. He was assigned to develop a night-fighter unit to deal with the fledgling British night-bomber attacks in 1940. Kammhuber proved

to be an exceptionally talented commander both in creating this novel and extremely technical form of fighter force, and also in overseeing the erection of an elaborate, radar-based early warning network. His influence waned in the summer of 1943 after the British began electronic warfare against the German radar network, and he ran afoul of other Luftwaffe leaders by trying to expand the night-fighter force at the expense of other branches. He was pushed aside in November 1943, shuffled off to Luftflotte 5 in Norway. Kammhuber's corps was renamed as I Jagdkorps and Generalleutnant Josef "Beppo" Schmid took command. Schmid had headed the intelligence section of the Luftwaffe general staff during the Battle of Britain with unimpressive results. He subsequently led the Luftwaffe's "Hermann Göring" Panzer Division before being appointed to the Reich defense command. His performance in the new post was viewed favorably enough in Berlin that in December 1944 he was given command of Luftwaffenkommando West, which controlled all the air units supporting the western front.

Kammhuber's role as night-fighter inspector was also eliminated when both the night- and day-fighter positions were rolled into a single fighter inspectorate under Generalleutnant Adolf Galland. He was a fighter *Staffel* (the equivalent of a squadron) commander before the war, and won fame as commander of Jagdgeschwader 26 in the Battle of Britain, where he became an ace and won the Knight's Cross. In 1942 Galland became the youngest Luftwaffe *Generalmajor* at the age of 30, serving as General der Jagdflieger (Inspector of Fighters). He was a foe of Jeschonnek and a constant irritant to Göring because of his obsessive championing of the fighter force. He allied himself with Milch to help promote an expansion of fighter production. Galland was instrumental in the various tactical and weapons innovations developed in 1943–44 to deal with the USAAF bomber threat, but he was too brash and insufficiently deferential to the top Nazi leaders to proceed any further in the Luftwaffe hierarchy.

AMERICAN COMMANDERS

At the Casablanca conference in 1943 command of the Combined Bomber Offensive was assigned to **Air Chief Marshal Charles Portal** of the RAF. Portal's sensitive political goal was to attempt to coordinate the divergent tactical approaches of Harris's RAF Bomber Command and Spaatz's United States Strategic Air Forces (USSTAF) during Operation *Pointblank*.

LEFT
The two senior Allied air commanders were USAAF commander Gen. Henry "Hap" Arnold on the left and RAF Air Chief Marshal Charles Portal on the right. (NARA)

RIGHT
The senior Allied bomber commanders in 1943 were Air Marshal Arthur Harris of RAF Bomber Command on the left and Lt. Gen. Ira Eaker, Eighth Air Force commander, on the right. (NARA)

From an American perspective, the key commander was **General Henry "Hap" Arnold**, Commanding General, Army Air Force. Arnold was a driving force behind the USAAF's doctrine of strategic bombing, and he was deeply involved in the *Pointblank* operation. He graduated from the US Military Academy at West Point in 1907 and had been a flight student at the Wright Flying School. He was a pioneer in the fledgling USAAF before World War I, and became Chief of the Air Corps in 1938. As a member of the US Joint Chiefs of Staff and the Allied Combined Chiefs of Staff he played a critical role in establishing American and Allied strategic plans.

The Eighth Air Force was commanded by **Lieutenant-General Ira Eaker** from December 1942. He served in Army aviation units in the 1920s and was involved in a number of the early record-breaking flights. Eaker was a close associate of Hap Arnold and in the late 1930s they jointly authored several books promoting the Army Air Corps. In 1941 he was assigned to special duty with the RAF to observe British tactics and doctrine, and in January 1942 he was appointed commanding general for the bomber command of United States Army Forces in the British Isles (USAFBI), the initial version of what would emerge at the end of the year as the Eighth Air Force. Arnold was not entirely satisfied with Eaker's performance in the autumn of 1943, being particularly distressed by the low readiness rates of the bombers. At the end of 1943 Arnold decided to shift Eaker to take control of the Mediterranean Allied Air Forces in Italy.

In his place came **Lieutenant-General Carl Spaatz**. Spaatz graduated from West Point in 1914 and commanded the 31st Aero Squadron in France in 1917. Spaatz and Eaker were copilots on the record-breaking *Question Mark* endurance flight in January 1929, which pioneered aerial refueling. He was heavily involved in early bomber development, commander of 7th Bombardment Group at Rockwell Field in 1929–31, and Arnold's executive

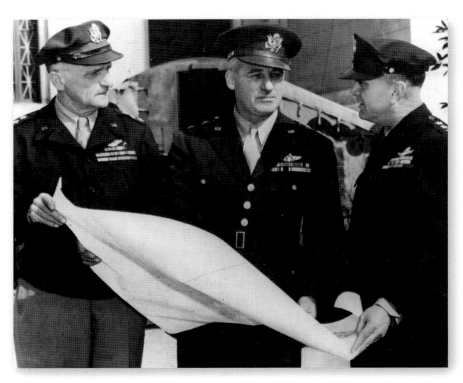

The senior American bomber commanders after the reorganization in February 1944 were (left to right): commander of the USSTAF, Lt. Gen. Carl Spaatz; commander of the Fifteenth Air Force in Italy, Maj. Gen. Nathan Twining; and commander of the Mediterranean Allied Air Force, Maj. Gen. Ira Eaker. (NARA)

officer at March Field airbase before the war. He served as a special observer with the RAF in 1940 and preceded Eaker as Eighth Air Force commander before being sent to lead the Twelfth Air Force in combat in the North Africa, Sicily, and Italy campaigns from December 1942 to the end of 1943. In February 1944 the strategic air forces in Europe were reorganized; the Eighth Air Force headquarters was redesignated as United States Strategic Air Forces (USSTAF) with Spaatz controlling both the Eighth and Fifteenth Air Forces.

As a result of this change, there was a need for another Eighth Air Force commander, and **Lieutenant-General James Doolittle** was selected. Doolittle was among the most recognized USAAF commanders during the war. He was a well-known aviation pioneer in the 1920s, winning the Schneider Trophy in 1925 and making the first "blind" flight (using instruments only) in 1929; he was also an influential pioneer in aeronautical engineering and played a key role in promoting the production of high-octane aviation fuel. He won his greatest fame for leading the volunteer squadron on the raid on Tokyo on April 18, 1942, for which he was decorated with the Medal of Honor. He commanded Fifteenth Air Force in Italy shortly before being reassigned to Britain.

Doolittle's Fifteenth Air Force command went to **Major-General Nathan Twining.** Twining was chief of staff of the US Army Forces South Pacific in July 1942–43, and it was his excellent performance as commander of the Thirteenth Air Force based in the Solomon Islands in 1943 that attracted Arnold's attention. Although the operations in the Pacific were in many ways different to those in Europe, Arnold was impressed with Twining's ability to keep his bombers flying even out of primitive airbase conditions in the tropical Pacific.

The Eighth Air Force had associated bomber and fighter commands. The VIII Bomber Command had been commanded by **Major-General Frederick Anderson,** and when this headquarters was converted to the Eighth Air Force in February 1944 Spaatz retained Anderson as deputy for operations. The VIII Fighter Command post had been more contentious. It had been led by **Brigadier-General Frank Hunter** until the end of August 1943. Eaker was unhappy with Hunter's preference for fighter sweeps over bomber escort, and he was feeling heat from Hap Arnold to push on long-range escort fighters. Hunter was replaced by **Major-General William Kepner.** Kepner had been involved in the USAAF's range-extension program earlier in 1943, and he would oversee many of the critical technical and tactical innovations that would change the course of Operation *Pointblank*, including the use of disposable fuel tanks and the introduction of the P-51 Mustang in the escort role.

OPPOSING FORCES

LUFTWAFFE

The Reich defense command was originally designated as Luftwaffen-befehlshaber Mitte (LBM: Luftwaffe Command Center). The Reich defenses included day-fighter and night-fighter divisions as well as flak divisions and brigades. Besides the fighter units based in Germany, it also controlled the forward-deployed units along the "bomber autobahn" over the Netherlands, so called because it was the route along which most Allied bombers travelled in order to reach their targets. The tactical fighter units deployed in France were under the separate command of Luftflotte 3 in Paris, and these units were also heavily involved in interception missions against USAAF bombers. In March 1943 General Kammhuber attempted to consolidate these units under a single command. The Luftflotte 3 commander, Generalfeldmarschall Hugo Sperrle, forcefully argued that Luftflotte 3's main mission would be to defeat an Allied invasion of France, and therefore he was able to fend off attempts to absorb his fighter units under the Reich defense command.

Through the beginning of 1943, Reich air defense was based primarily on flak and night-fighters, since the main threat was from RAF night attacks. Germany deployed the most lavish flak forces in the world, and in the first quarter of 1943 flak accounted for 90 of 186 Allied bombers shot down and

The Luftwaffe's ground-control-interception system was based around the "Battle Opera Houses." This is a wartime artist's impression of the 3. Jagddivision command post at Deelen in the Netherlands in 1944, codenamed "Diogenes." The division commander, his staff and associated liaison officers (1) sit above and behind the banks of fighter-direction officers (*Jägerleitoffiziere*) who controlled the fighter squadrons by radio. The main situation map (2) kept track of the location and direction of approaching bomber formations (5, 6, and 7). The main situation map was supported by a separate reference map group (8), which kept track of friendly fighters by means of the Y-Combat System. They passed this data to signals troops at the back of the room (3) who plotted the positions on the main map using light projectors, along with data from the threat-tracking staff above (4). (MHI)

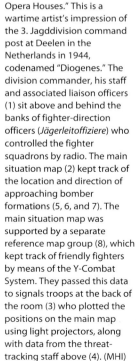

Flak dispositions, June 1944

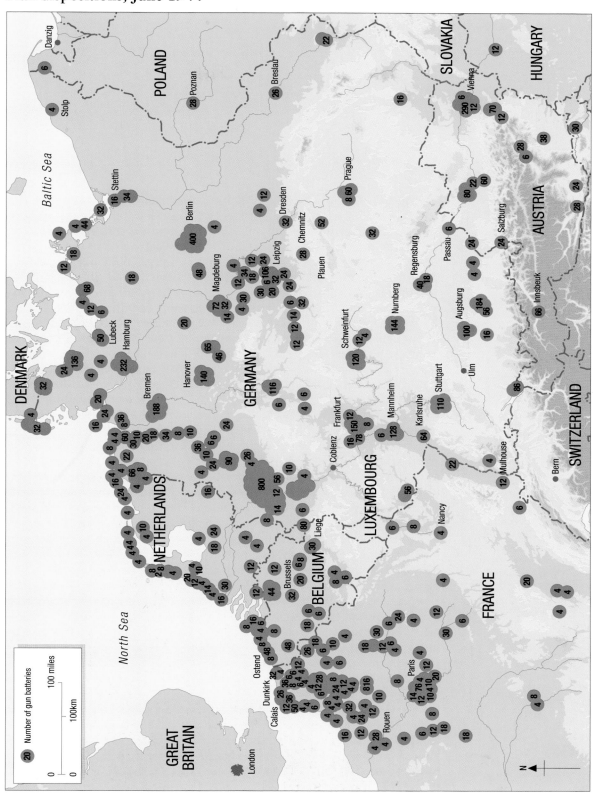

724 of 805 destroyed. The flak defenses were enormously complex and expensive, requiring not only an extensive array of complex heavy artillery, but also an associated fire-control system based on searchlights and acoustic sensors, and later relying on radar. In 1943 flak constituted 29 percent of the German weapons budget and 20 percent of the munitions budget, and the flak force included half of all Luftwaffe personnel.

The flak force was regionally organized under the *Luftgau* commands, which were regional administrations roughly paralleling the Army's *Wehrkreis* military districts. The *Luftgau* commands were responsible for raising and training Luftwaffe personnel, administering airbases on their territory, and operating the regional flak units. There were six of these districts in the Reich, and at the end of 1943 they controlled 9 flak divisions and 4 separate flak brigades, or about 60 percent of the total flak force; Luftflotte 3 on the approaches to the Reich had a further 3 divisions and 3 separate brigades. In 1943 the Reich flak units nearly doubled from 629 heavy flak batteries in January 1943 to 1,300 in January 1944.

In spite of their earlier infatuation with flak, there was growing disquiet amongst senior Nazi leaders over the enormous costs of the flak force and its meager results during the RAF's devastating summer 1943 Ruhr campaign. Flak was even less crucial in the battle against American daytime bombers, accounting for only about a quarter of US bomber losses in 1942–43. American commanders had a somewhat different view of the flak threat, recognizing the smaller numbers of bomber losses attributable to flak alone, but more aware of the significant number of stragglers damaged by flak and then shot down by fighters. Furthermore, flak intimidated bomber crews and played a crucial role in degrading bomber accuracy. The flak commanders continued to push for upgrades in their armament, especially the trend from using the 88mm to the 105mm and 128mm guns because of their greater reach. Nevertheless, the growing threat of USAAF daytime-bomber attacks forced the Luftwaffe to place more emphasis on fighters over flak, and this was recognized by organization changes in early 1944. The previous Luftwaffenbefehlshaber Mitte was transformed into Luftflotte Reich on February 5, 1944.

The Reich fighter force was dominated by night-fighter units through 1943, since the principal threat was from RAF Bomber Command. The day- and night-fighter units in Germany were subordinated to Kammhuber's XII Fliegerkorps, which had its forward headquarters at Zeist near Utrecht in the Netherlands. The initial USAAF bomber raids against the U-boat bases on the Bay of Biscay were mostly intercepted by fighters from Luftflotte 3 based in France and Belgium. At the beginning of 1943 the Reich day-fighter force was quite small, consisting mainly of Jagdgeschwader 1 with two *Gruppen* deployed forward in the Netherlands and two more on the German Bight covering the North Sea harbors and shipyards. As USAAF air raids increased through the spring of 1943, the Reich defense force was expanded in an ad hoc fashion by activating training and factory units for local daytime defense. The better-armed night-fighter units were used reluctantly in daytime missions against USAAF bombers, but these units were a precious asset because of their costly equipment and highly trained crews. As a result, Zerstörer Geschwader 26 and Zerstörer Geschwader 76 were reconstituted for Reich defense by recreating disbanded squadrons and drawing back heavy-fighter squadrons to Germany, mostly from the Mediterranean theater.

The fighter force was organized on a regional basis under the control of a *Jagddivision* (fighter division). In 1943–44 there were five of these involved in the defense of the Reich, supplemented by two more with Luftflotte 3 in France on the approaches to the Reich. These divisions were of mixed composition, including both day- and night-fighter *Geschwader* (wings), and each division also controlled three or four *Nachrichten Regimenten* (surveillance regiments), which operated the regional radar and sensor networks. A fighter *Geschwader* was roughly equivalent to a USAAF group, and they were classified by type: *Jagdgeschwader* (JG; day fighter), *Zerstörerjagdgeschwader* (ZG: heavy fighter), and *Nachtjagdgeschwader*, (NG: night fighter). The *Geschwader* was organized as three *Gruppen*; a *Gruppe* was in turn broken down into *Staffeln* and then *Schwadrone*. The divisions did not control a specific number or type of *Geschwader*, but were primarily command-and-control organizations with fighter units being moved around by higher commands as the campaign warranted. As a result, the sub-units of each *Geschwader* were not necessarily subordinated to a single division. For example, in February 1944 Jagdgeschwader 11 had most of its *Staffeln* subordinated to 3. Jagddivision in northwest Germany, but three with neighboring 2. Jagddivision in Denmark. The fighter divisions took on an increasingly important role in managing the Reich air-defense network, and by the end of 1943 and the beginning of 1944 an integrated air-defense system was maturing.

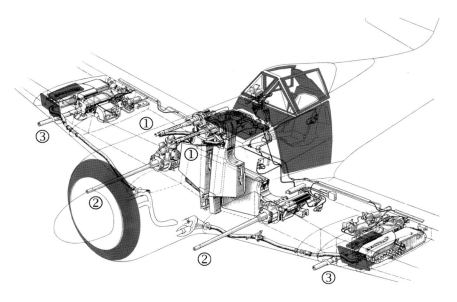

The weak armament on Luftwaffe fighters in late 1942 and early 1943 led to an improvement program to deal with the American heavy bombers. This illustration based on the original handbook drawings shows the new armament package for the Fw 190A-7/R 2, A-8/R 2, and A-9/R8 Sturmflugzeug. A pair of 13mm MG 131 were substituted for the original pair of 7.92mm MG 17 machine guns over the engine (1). The 20mm MG 151s in the wing roots (2) remained the same, but a pair of powerful 30mm MK 108s were added in the wing (3). The special Sturmbock versions for new *Sturmstaffel* close-range-attack units added armor plating around the pilot, the engine oil cooler ring, and the 30mm guns as shown here by the shaded areas. (Author's collection)

The twin-engine heavy fighters like this Bf 110G-2 from Zerstörergeschwader 26 could accommodate a pair of 21cm rocket launchers under both wings. Here, an officer is supervising the loading of a rocket into the launch tube. (NARA)

The Luftnachrichten Dienst (Air Surveillance Service) provided the Luftwaffe's early warning and tracking units. In its most basic form it consisted of visual-observation posts linked to an aircraft-reporting center (Fluko: Flugwachekommando). In 1939–43, radars and other electronic sensors were added to this network, evolving into a sophisticated network, dubbed the Kammhuber Line by the Allies, named after General Josef Kammhuber. The first layer of the improved system was the Funkaufklärungsdienst (Electronic Intelligence Early Warning Service), which monitored the radio channels used by Allied bomber formations during the preparatory phases of the missions, during which the aircraft were flying over England; by 1943 the system was expanded to include sensors such as at Samos and Fano, which monitored additional electronic emissions such as those from aircraft radars. The initial data was fed to the Seeräuber (Pirate) center at Zeist in the Netherlands, which distributed it to the other command posts. The next layer consisted of long-range search radars, such as the Mammut and Wassermann types, located along the French and Dutch coasts. These picked up the Allied bombers as they crossed the Channel and the target data was handed over to the belts of forward-alert radar centers with the smaller Freya and Würzburg radars, which continued to track the bombers as they approached and entered German airspace.

In 1942–43 the data from these surveillance units was fed to a variety of small tactical command posts operated by the flak, *Luftgau*, and fighter units. The fighter units used this data as the basis for their ground-control-intercept (GCI) network for the night-fighter campaign against the RAF bombers. About three fourths of all night interceptions resulted in a bomber kill, and the interceptions were extremely dependent upon the night fighters being vectored into a precise area by means of radar-directed ground control. The Nachtjagdraumführer (or NaFü: night fighter director) system was a regionally based GCI network with individual stations controlling their assigned night fighters. The 1942–43 network was adequate for directing night fighters, but by the summer of 1943 it was becoming overwhelmed by the need to also provide all-day fighter control to the day-fighter force in their new battles with the USAAF. The head of the Luftwaffe signals branch, General der Luftwaffe Wolfgang Martini, began a reorganization of the early warning network in the spring of 1943 that attempted to address these concerns as well as deal with the emerging threat of Allied electronic warfare. These improvements were concentrated along the "bomber autobahn," along which most RAF and USAAF bombers passed.

In the autumn of 1943 a series of organization changes were made to reorient the fighter force from its focus on night fighters to an all-day interceptor force. On September 15, 1943, XII Fliegerkorps was renamed I Jagdkorps; Kammhuber remained in charge of the night-fighter force but Generalleutnant Josef "Beppo" Schmid took over the corps command. As before, 7. Jagddivision in central-southern Germany remained autonomous from I Jagdkorps, which complicated fighter control once US bombers began to penetrate deeper into central and southern Germany in 1944. As part of the reforms, the *Nachtjagdraumführer* system gave way to a *Jagdabschnittsführer* (Fighter Sector Director) system, marking the switch to all-day radar and GCI coverage. Complaints by fighter commanders about delays in the transfer of radar information led to a transfer of the command of the *Luftnachrichten* (air surveillance) regiments controlling the radars from the corps headquarters in Zeist to the regional *Jagddivision* headquarters. This was another step in the direction of a more responsive though less centralized air-defense system, culminating in February 1944 when new *Jagddivision* command centers became responsible for creating a common air-situation report (*Luftlagebild*) instead of the confusing mix of flak, fighter, and *Luftgau* reports that had existed previously. The fighter sector directors were subordinated to the new divisional command posts and remained in control of the peripheral sectors, as noted in the accompanying order of battle here. The new divisional command posts were highly sophisticated data-collection and dissemination stations, derisively called "battle opera houses" by the fighter pilots for their elaborately choreographed activities. Data from the radar stations and other

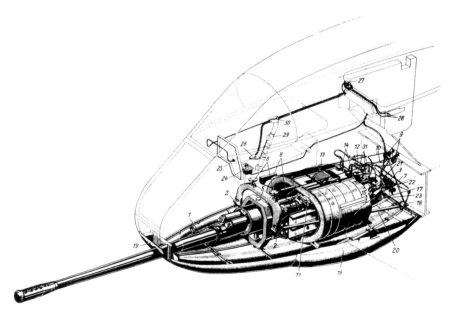

To extend the stand-off range of the armament of the Me-410 heavy fighter, the 50mm Bordkanone was mounted in the Me-410A-1/U4 starting in October 1943 and later on the Me-410B-2/U4. After a test example was displayed to Hitler, it became one of his high-priority pet projects. The gun was derived from the PaK 38 antitank gun, modified with a pneumatically-powered 22-round autoloader located under the pilot's seat. In practice, the weapon proved very delicate in combat use, though a single hit could knock down a B-17. By the time this weapon entered service in the early spring of 1944, the Me-410 was too vulnerable to American escort fighters to survive. (NARA)

sources were fed to the posts, the data was collated and the air-situation report created, which was then used by the fighter director to assign missions to the division's various fighter units.

Direction of the fighters was conducted by voice radio from the fighter control center (*Jägerleit Gefechtstand*) at the division command post. The key link between the ground-control-intercept system on the ground and the fighters in the air was the Y-Combat System (*Y-Vehrfahren-Kampf*), better known by its codename of 'Benito'. The system's FuS AN 733 ground stations interacted with a FuG16ZY transponder on the fighter, which retransmitted the signal back to the ground, allowing the Y-Station to track friendly fighters. Not all fighters had this equipment, often only a single fighter per squadron. During the 1944 air campaign this system was gradually compromised by Allied electronic jamming.

The Luftwaffe's ground-control-intercept system came under increasing stress in the summer and autumn of 1943 because of the Allies' introduction of radar countermeasures, starting with the RAF's use of "window" in July 1943 followed by the similar USAAF use of "chaff." These were metalized strips dropped from the bombers to create artificial clouds that interfered with radar's ability to distinguish the bombers. This electronic countermeasure could be used both to disguise the true identity, size, and location of the bomber force from the early warning radars, and also as a decoy to create a false target or to interfere with the fire-direction radars used by the flak sites. In addition, the Allies began a very active campaign of electronic jamming, not only of the radars, but also attacking various links in the command chain such as the radio channels between the fighter direction centers and the fighters. One expedient method used to circumvent the growing electronic warfare threat was the use of *Fühlungshalter* "shadow" aircraft, which flew alongside American bomber formations and reported their course, altitude, and direction. By late 1943, the *Jagddivisionen* each had at least one shadow unit, usually using Ju-88C heavy fighters adapted to the role.

Defense of the Reich order of battle, February 1944*

Luftflotte Reich	Berlin	Generaloberst Hans-Jürgen Stumpff
I Jagdkorps	**Zeist**	**Generalmajor Josef Schmid**
1. Jagddivision	Döberitz	Oberst Günther Lützow
Jagdabschnittsführer-Ostpreussen	Insterburg	Oberstleutnant Karl-Gottfried Nordmann
Jagdabschnittsführer-Schlesien	Cosel	Oberstleutnant Hans-Hugo Witt
2. Jagddivision	Stade	Generalmajor Max-Josef Ibel
Jagdabschnittsführer-Dänemark	Grove	Major Müller-Rendsberg
3. Jagddivision	Deelen (Netherlands)	Generalmajor Walter Grabmann
Jagdabschnittsführer-Mittelrhein	Darmstadt	Oberst Truebenbach
7. Jagddivision	Schleissheim	Generalmajor Joachim-Friedrich Huth
Jagdabschnittsführer Ostmark	Vienna-Cobenzl	Oberst Hendrix
30. Jagddivision	Berlin	Oberst Hajo Hermann
Luftgaukommando I	**Königsberg**	**General der Flieger Hellmuth Bieneck**
Luftgaukommando III	**Berlin**	**General der Flak Gerhard Hoffmann**
1. Flak Division	Berlin	Generalleutnant Erich Kressmann
14. Flak Division	Leipzig	Generalleutnant Rudolf Schulze
Luftgaukommando VI	**Münster**	**Generalmajor August Schmidt**
4. Flak Division	Duisberg	Generalleutnant Johannes Hintz
7. Flak Division	Cologne	Generalmajor Heinrich Burchard
22. Flak Division	Dortmund	Generalmajor Friedrich Römer
Luftgaukommando VII	**Munich**	**General der Flak Emil Zenetti**
4. Flak Brigade	Munich	Generalmajor Ernst Uhl
20. Flak Brigade	Stuttgart	Oberst Wolfgang Bayer
Luftgaukommando VIII	**Krakow**	**General der Flak Walter Sommé**
15. Flak Brigade	Posen	Oberst Oskar Krämer
Luftgaukommando XI	**Hamburg**	**General der Flieger Ludwig Wolff**
3. Flak Division	Hamburg	Generalmajor Alwin Wolz
8. Flak Division	Bremen	Generalleutnant Kurt Wagner
8. Flak Brigade	Wismar	Oberst Ernst Martin
15. Flak Brigade	Hanover	Oberst Oskar Krämer
Luftgaukommando XII	**Wiesbaden**	**General der Flak Fritz Heilingbrunner**
21. Flak Division	Darmstadt	Generalleutnant Kurt Stüdemann
21. Flak Brigade	Nuremburg	Oberst Hans Jürgens
Luftgaukommando XVII	**Vienna**	**General der Flieger Dörstling**
24. Flak Division	Vienna	Generalmajor Fritz Grieshammer

Does not include the fighter and flak units of Luftflotte 3 headquartered in Paris with the 4. and 5. Jagddivisionen

The Reich defense force continued to expand through 1943, though hardly enough to keep pace with Allied growth. The expansion of the single-engine day-fighter force for Reich defense came partly at the expense of the Russian and Mediterranean fronts and partly from increased fighter production and pilot training; transfers from the Russian and Mediterranean fronts each accounted for about a quarter of the increase and the remaining half from new units. It should also be noted that the growth of the Reich defense fighter force was severely constrained by the high loss rate in this theater. Although the Western Front averaged about 55 percent of the Luftwaffe single-engine fighter deployments in 1943–44, this area suffered 65 percent of total losses.

Luftwaffe fighter deployment, December 1942 to June 1944

	12/31/42	3/30/43	6/30/43	9/30/43	12/31/43	3/31/44	6/30/44
Single-engine day fighter	380	530	499	431	346	392	414
Twin-engine day fighter	36	56	41	9	16	13	18
Twin-engine night fighter	3	17	0	65	66	75	118
Russian Front sub-total	419	603	540	505	428	480	550
Single-engine day fighter	212	336	493	236	318	267	125
Twin-engine day fighter	55	103	103	9	9	24	22
Twin-engine night fighter	13	37	39	23	34	35	0
Mediterranean Front sub-total	280	476	635	268	361	326	147
Defense of the Reich							
Single-engine day fighter	651	336	413	643	562	853	448
Twin-engine day fighter	14	36	2	273	196	110	161
Twin-engine night fighter	379	460	512	497	464	454	549
Germany sub-total	1,044	832	927	1,413	1,222	1,417	1,158
Single-engine day fighter	0	302	404	340	309	166	526
Twin-engine day fighter	0	0	11	101	69	104	41
Twin-engine night fighter	0	0	0	0	52	52	136
Western Front sub-total	0	302	415	441	430	322	703
Total (All Fronts)	1,743	2,213	2,517	2,627	2,441	2,545	2,558
Percent of Reich Defense (all types)	59.8	51.2	53.3	70.5	67.6	68.3	72.7
Percent of Reich Defense (day fighters)	49.3	39.6	42.2	66.4	62.2	63.9	67.0

The single-engine day fighters available for Reich defense in early 1943 were mostly Bf-109G and Fw-190A tactical fighters. They were not ideal as bomber interceptors because of their weak armament, which was a pair of 13mm machine guns and a single 20mm cannon on the Bf-109G-6 and a somewhat heavier two 13mm and four 20mm cannon on the Fw-190A-3. These were inadequate against an adversary as sturdy as the B-17 bomber, a fact evident in their early kill rates, which were only about 2.3 kills per 100 attacks in 1942. The machine guns were almost useless against a B-17 and a German study concluded that on average it took 20 20mm hits to shoot down a B-17. Since only about 2 percent of the rounds fired actually hit, this implied

An important innovation in flak defense was the use of mobile railroad batteries. This allowed a portion of the force to be kept in mobile reserve and then shifted to various localities when the focus of Allied bombing changed. The most common configuration was the Geschützwagen III(E), which had ammunition-stowage bins on either side of the gun. It was used with both the 88mm and the 105mm gun, the latter of which is seen here. (NARA)

that it took 23 seconds of firing to down a B-17, an impossible duration under the circumstances, barring a few lucky hits. Steps were already under way to deploy the powerful MK 108 30mm cannon on the fighters, but its production rate was still low. A German study concluded that it took only three 30mm hits on average to down a B-17.

The difficulty of the single-engine fighters in dealing with the bombers led to increased use of twin-engine Zerstörer heavy fighters, starting in the autumn of 1943 with the commitment of Zerstörergeschwader 26 and Zerstörergeschwader 76 to Reich defense. These two heavy-fighter units were primarily equipped with the Bf-110G-2 and G-3, although Zerstörergeschwader 26 also operated the Ju-88C6. The new Me-410 began to be issued to these units in October 1943, eventually becoming the predominant type by the spring of 1944.

In the spring of 1943, Erprobungskommando 25 (Test Command 25) was created to develop armament to deal with the heavy bombers, including heavy cannons and rockets. Besides this effort, some German units experimented on their own initiative. The first improvised attempt at air-to-air bombing took place on February 16, 1943, during the raid on St Nazaire, and the USAAF recorded at least nine more bomb attacks in May 1943 and several more in June before it tapered off because of ineffectiveness. A more peculiar approach was to troll through a bomber formation with a bomb tethered to a cable, but this tactic proved ineffective and was quickly dropped.

In the short term, the most important innovation was the deployment of air-to-air rockets. These could be quickly introduced since they were readily adaptable from army Nebelwerfer artillery rockets with a time fuse added. They allowed the day-fighters to engage the B-17 from outside the lethal range of their .50-cal machine guns. Several types were tested and issued on an experimental basis starting in April 1943, but the predominant type was the 21cm WGr. 42, which was first encountered during the mission over Wilhelmshaven on May 21, 1943. This rocket required minimum modification to existing fighters beyond a simple launch tube and could be fitted to single-engine fighters (two launchers) as well as heavy fighters (four launchers).

An often-overlooked aspect of flak defense is the extensive deployment of Kriegsmarine flak batteries along the Dutch and French coast, which were usually the first to engage bomber streams heading to targets in Germany. This is one of the more common types, the 105mm SKC C/32 on MPL C/30 mount with a *Deckenschutzschild* armored cupola. A Kommandogerät 41L optical rangefinder in an armored cupola can be seen behind the center turret. These belonged to 2./MaFlAbt 819 (2nd Battery, Naval Flak Regiment 819) stationed at La Renardière near Toulon, which had numerous engagements with bombers of the Fifteenth Air Force. (NARA)

The main disadvantage of the rockets was that the drag of the launch tubes degraded fighter performance, but this did not become a major issue until the advent of Allied escort fighters. The rockets were not especially accurate but they were extremely effective in breaking up the tight B-17 box formations, which then made it easier for the fighters to press home their gun attacks.

Besides the internal MK 108 30mm cannon, a variety of new cannon were added under the wings of the single-engine fighters, for example, the Bf-109G-6/R-4 "gunboat" with two MG 108 30mm cannon and the Bf-109G-6/R-6 with two MG 151 20mm cannon, which began to enter service in the summer of 1943. The "R" suffix on the fighter designation stood for "Rüsatz" and indicated which field-modification kit had been added to the fighter. A variety of automatic cannon were also adapted for the heavy fighters, including the 37mm Flak 18 and Flak 36 and an aircraft version of the 50mm antitank gun with a new automatic loader. The increasing firepower was evident in US reports, which noted a ratio of 40 cannon hits per 100 machine-gun hits in 1942, but 77 cannon hits per hundred machine-gun hits in the first half of 1943.

Besides technical innovations, new tactics were also developed. After a few encounters with the B-17F in 1942, German fighter pilots realized that its forward armament was weak and that a few hits on the cockpit were often lethal. As a result, units began to use head-on attacks in late 1942. By the spring of 1943, this had been refined into the dreaded "12 o'clock high" tactic, where the fighters attacked in a slow, shallow dive to minimize the closing speed and increase the chances of actually hitting the bomber. The idea of suicide ramming attacks was broached but quickly rejected. Instead, the idea emerged of creating an armored version of the Fw-190 that would be used to press home attacks at closer range. This led to the formation of Sturmstaffel 1 in June 1943 and the gradual addition of special attack squadrons in every fighter *Geschwader*. The other important change was to concentrate the fighter squadrons into larger formations and to attack simultaneously and en masse; the innovations in ground-control-intercept mentioned earlier made this possible. The improvements in weapons, firepower, and tactics substantially increased the lethality of German fighters in their encounters with the B-17. The rate of kills per engagement rose from 2.3 kills per hundred attacks in late 1942 to 3.6 kills by mid 1943, 5 kills by late 1943 and to a high of 17.7 kills by the spring of 1944.

Germany was very slow in shifting toward a defensive priority in aircraft production, especially single-engine day fighters, until it was too late. This is detailed below in "Opposing Plans." Even though German aircraft production kept ahead of attrition through most of 1943, the Luftwaffe had a difficult time translating the new aircraft surplus in 1944 into new fighter units. The main bottleneck was training. This resulted from endemic fuel shortages, which only grew worse with time, limiting the number of flight hours available. To stretch this finite resource, the Luftwaffe chose quantity over quality, continuously cutting back on flight-training time. As a result, 1,662 new single-seat fighter pilots were trained in 1942, increasing to 3,276 trained in 1943. But training fell from about 200 hours in late 1942–early 1943 to about 175 hours in mid 1943–44. In contrast, Allied training actually increased and averaged 320 hours or more. The discrepancy was greatest in flight time on operational types (i.e. non-training aircraft), with Luftwaffe pilots' hours falling from about 40 hours to 30 while USAAF pilots went from about 75 hours to 125 hours. The training limitations also affected trained ground crews. On average it took about 160 Luftwaffe ground personnel for every pilot, and skilled mechanics and other specialists were also in very short supply, which adversely impacted readiness rates and limited the Luftwaffe's ability to create more fighter units.

USAAF

The USAAF's original strategic force in the ETO was the Eighth Air Force. Based in England, it was a self-contained force with its own bomber, escort-fighter, and support elements. Its VIII Bomber Command was originally organized into three wings, later expanding into three divisions. Its fighter element was VIII Fighter Command. In the autumn of 1943, after bases had been secured in Italy, the Fifteenth Air Force was deployed in Italy to take part in Operation *Pointblank*. As mentioned earlier, the strategic-bombing effort was centralized under Lt. Gen. Carl Spaatz's USSTAF, which managed the operations of both the Eighth and Fifteenth Air Forces. The Eighth Air Force remained larger than the Fifteenth Air Force, with nearly double the aircraft.

The next organizational level below this was the bombardment divisions, with three in the Eighth Air Force in 1944. The divisions were based around several bombardment wings supported by a fighter wing for escort support; the wings in turn consisted of groups. The group was the smallest autonomous unit within the USAAF and during 1943–45 a Bombardment Group (Heavy) consisted of three or four squadrons. In the autumn of 1943 groups had an authorized establishment of 35 aircraft plus a reserve, but later in the war a four-squadron bombardment group would have a paper strength of 48 B-17 or B-24 bombers.

The actual tactical formation most commonly used was the combat-box formation. The initial practice in 1942 was to attack in elements of three bombers, though by early 1943 this had evolved into squadrons of six bombers. As the intensity of German fighter opposition increased, by April 1943 the small formations gave way to loose boxes of 12–14 bombers widely spaced to permit evasive action. By May 1943 the standard formation for each group was a tight combat box of 18–21 bombers to maximize the defensive firepower of the bombers. A combat box was about 850ft (260m) in altitude, 900ft (275m) in breadth and 600ft (185m) in trail. The next level of tactical deployment was the combat-wing formation, which consisted of three staggered combat boxes.

BANDITS, 1 O'CLOCK LOW!

An element of P-51B Mustang fighters (1) of the 363rd Squadron, 357th Fighter Group, peel off to intercept a group of Fw 190 fighters (2) attempting to intercept a B-17 formation above (3) during the March 1944 air battles. The P-51B in the foreground (4) is flown by Flight Officer Chuck Yeager, who later went on to fame as the first pilot to break the sound barrier in the Bell X-1 rocket plane. This particular aircraft carries the name "Glamourus Glen" (5), a misspelling of the intended "Glamorous Glennis," named after Yeager's girlfriend and later wife, Glennis Dickhouse. Yeager was shot down while flying this aircraft (B6*Y s/n 43-6763) on March 5, 1944, on his eighth mission, but he evaded capture with the help of a French Resistance network and escaped to Spain over the Pyrenees mountains later that month. He returned to England to continue flying Mustangs, and was credited with 11.5 victories by war's end, including a

Me-262 jet fighter. The Mustang immediately above Yeager's is Captain Clarence "Bud" Anderson's "Old Crow" (6). Anderson ended the war with 16.25 victories.

Although the P-51B had an excellent radius of action, the addition of a pair of 75-gallon drop tanks (7) enabled the Mustang to fly deep into Germany. It was the practice to keep these tanks in place until the fuel was exhausted, but the fighters would release the tanks (8) on contact with enemy fighters because of the hazard they presented in a dogfight, both from their drag and their flammability. Compared with German fighters like the Fw 190, the P-51B was not especially well armed, with four .50-cal machine guns, but this was adequate as the P-51 was fighting enemy fighters, not heavy bombers. The later P-51D had six .50-cal machine guns while the P-47D had eight.

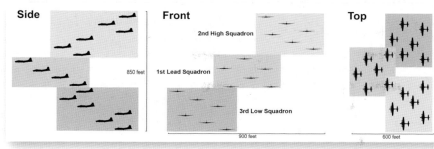

Side

Front

2nd High Squadron

Top

850 feet

1st Lead Squadron

3rd Low Squadron

900 feet

600 feet

The USAAF employed a combat-box formation to maximize the defensive firepower of its heavy bombers. This is a typical mid-1943 formation for a bomber group with three squadrons. (Author's collection)

The Eighth Air Force was originally equipped with the Boeing B-17E and B-17F Flying Fortress heavy bombers. After the Luftwaffe discovered the weakness of the B-17's forward armament to front attacks, a series of improvements were made, first by mounting additional .50-cal machine guns in the nose of the B-17 and adding a Bendix twin .50-cal power turret on the new B-17G. Likewise, the importance of the tail position led to a substantial redesign during B-17G production, with the addition of the Cheyenne "semi-turret" in the rear. The machine guns on each bomber consumed a prodigious amount of ammunition, totaling 72.3 million rounds in 1943–45, or roughly 12,000 rounds for every enemy fighter claimed. Since the gunnery claims tended to be grossly inflated, the actual consumption per kill was over 50,000 rounds. Nevertheless, even when failing to shoot down enemy fighters, the machine guns played an important defensive role since they discouraged German pilots from pressing home attacks to shorter ranges where they might have been more effective.

TOP

The B-24 Liberator equipped one of the Eighth Air Force's three divisions. This B-24J-55 of the 328th Squadron, 93rd Bombardment Group, is seen during a mission against Friedrichshafen in August 1944. It was lost over Belgium on September 21, 1944. (NARA)

BOTTOM

One of the key technical innovations in 1943 was the ground-search radar, which allowed targets to be attacked through cloud cover. This was the first B-17F fitted with the British H2S radar in a special fairing under the nose, and seen on August 25, 1943, while serving with the 92nd Bombardment Group. (NARA)

The B-17 was supplemented with the Consolidated B-24 Liberator in 1943, though the B-17 remained the predominant type in the USSTAF through 1944. The B-24 had a larger bomb capacity than the B-17, but many crews felt that the B-17 was a more durable aircraft. In the Eighth Air Force, 1st and 3rd Bombardment Divisions operated the B-17 and the 2nd Bombardment Division operated the B-24.

Besides the armament improvements, one of the most important technical innovations was the introduction of first-generation ground-scanning radars, starting with the British H2S "Stinkey" in the summer of 1943 on selected B-17 and B-24 "Pathfinders." The 482nd Bombardment Group at Alconbury was the center for Pathfinder activities. This radar could distinguish only the most reflective of radar targets, such as rivers, lakes, or large cities. Although not accurate enough for precision bombing, the radar did permit the USSTAF to conduct missions in overcast weather which had previously constrained bombing missions for much of the autumn and winter months. The H2S was followed by its improved American derivative, the H2X Mickey (AN/APS-15), starting with a nose-mounted pre-series version in October 1943 and the belly-mounted standard series in March 1944. Another electronic aid adopted in 1943 was the AN/APT-2 Carpet I radar jammer. This transmitter was designed to mask a bomber formation from Luftwaffe Würzburg fire-control radars by radiating electronic noise in the radar's operating frequency. When the Luftwaffe attempted to develop electronic counter-countermeasures (ECCM) in 1944 the USAAF deployed the APQ-9 Carpet III, which could conduct both barrage jamming and more focused spot jamming. A number of other electronic-warfare devices were fielded in 1943–44 to disrupt Luftwaffe fighter radios, GCI networks, and other communication and sensor nodes. By December 1943 each of the three bombardment divisions had their own Pathfinder squadron, and as more radars became available they were gradually deployed at wing and group level.

The H2S eventually made way for the more advanced H2X radar. These two B-17G Pathfinders from the 413th Squadron, 96th Bombardment Group, have their APS-15 Mickey (H2X) radars extended for use; the antenna took the place of the ventral ball turret. (NARA)

USAAF heavy-bomber strength, January–May 1944

Month	B-17s available	B-24s available	Subtotal	B-17s operational	B-24s operational	Subtotal
Eighth Air Force	938	244	1,182	657	186	843
Fifteenth Air Force	234	458	692	186	300	486
January	1,172	702	1,874	843	486	1,329
Eighth Air Force	1,129	352	1,481	786	260	1,046
Fifteenth Air Force	192	518	710	159	341	500
February	1,321	870	2,191	945	601	1,546
Eighth Air Force	1,100	399	1,499	792	302	1,094
Fifteenth Air Force	324	734	1,058	279	570	849
March	1,424	1,133	2,557	1,071	872	1,943
Eighth Air Force	1,129	485	1,614	908	379	1,287
Fifteenth Air Force	324	853	1,177	245	607	852
April	1,453	1,338	2,791	1,153	986	2,139
Eighth Air Force	1,190	836	2,026	949	675	1,624
Fifteenth Air Force	326	936	1,262	264	605	869
May	1,516	1,772	3,288	1,213	1,280	2,493

From late 1942 through the spring of 1943, both RAF and USAAF fighter units provided escort for the bombers. From its inception, the Eighth Air Force operated its own fighter groups, but a major mission for the fighter squadrons was fighter sweeps over France and the Low Countries. These were not especially effective from the standpoint of the number of German fighters destroyed, as the outnumbered German fighters soon learned to avoid the sweeps and focus their attention on intercepting bomber formations. Through the summer of 1943 the primary VIII Fighter Command aircraft was the Republic P-47C Thunderbolt. This had an effective combat radius of about 230 miles (370km), which enabled it to carry out shallow escort missions over Belgium and the Channel coast. While the longer-ranged Lockheed P-38 Lightning might have seemed a better choice for long-range escort, the Eighth Air Force's three assigned P-38 groups had been transferred to the Twelfth Air Force in October 1942 in support of North African operations. The P-38 was in heavy demand in the Pacific precisely because of its endurance, which greatly restricted the number available in Europe.

The first attempt to field a deep escort was the YB-40 destroyer escort aircraft, sometimes also called a heavy cruiser. This was a B-17 reinforced with additional machine-gun turrets as well as added armor plating. The first YB-40s arrived in Britain in May 1943 and were assigned to the 92nd Bombardment Group. Operational use of these aircraft in the summer of 1943 was very discouraging, as they did not add enough firepower to the combat box while at the same time the extra armor made them sluggish and they could not keep up with the other B-17s after they had dropped their bombs. The abrupt failure of the YB-40 led to its cancellation, along with the similar YB-41 based on the B-24; a scheme to use B-26 medium bombers

LEFT
One of the innovations during Operation *Pointblank* was the first combat trials of guided bombs. The GB-1 glide bomb used a small gyroscope to keep it on target. The main attraction of the glide bombs was that they could be released farther from the target than conventional bombs, permitting the bomber to avoid the worst concentrations of flak. Two were carried under each B-17, as seen here. After several failed attempts, the only "Grapefruit" mission took place during the attack on Cologne on May 28, 1944, with 115 dropped by B-17s of the 1st Bombardment Division. (NARA)

RIGHT
The first attempt at a long-range escort fighter was the YB-40, a B-17 bomber modified with double the number of machine guns and added armor. These are seen with the 91st Bombardment Group at Bassingbourne in May 1943, prior to their short-lived combat trials in the late spring and early summer of 1943. (NARA)

as escort fighters was also stillborn. One positive result from the YB-40 was proving the value of the chin-mounted Bendix turret, which was later adopted on the B-17G for forward defense.

In the meantime, the USAAF had been engaged in a development program to extend fighter range, prompted also by the long-range requirements of the Pacific theater and intercontinental ferrying operations. Two methods were under study: increasing the internal fuel capacity of existing fighters such as the P-38 and P-47, and developing external drop tanks. Of the two approaches, drop tanks presented the greatest engineering challenge since the USAAF sought a design that was bulletproof, lightweight, and sturdy enough that it could be pressurized so that the host fighter didn't require additional fuel pumps. Furthermore, since the tanks were disposable, the USAAF wanted them made from a non-strategic material at low cost. The Firestone 75-gallon tank passed firing trials in June 1942, and an enlarged 105-gallon type was developed. The Eighth Air Force first sought drop tanks in January 1943, and efforts began to have them fabricated by local industry in Britain. As a stopgap measure, in July 1943 VIII Fighter Command began distributing 200-gallon ferry tanks, which were not ideal for combat use but were useful in defining the requirement. The 75-gallon belly tank became available by July 1943, which extended the P-47's operating radius to 340 miles (550km), enough to reach northwestern Germany. They were first used on the mission to Kassel and Oschersleben on July 28, 1943, and won the overwhelming praise of the bomber crews. By August 1943, the enlarged 108-gallon belly tank was arriving, which extended the range to 375 miles (605km); by February 1944 the P-47 could be equipped with a 150-gallon belly tank (giving a 425-mile (685km) radius) or twin 108-gallon wing tanks (giving a 475-mile (765km) radius)

The slow pace of deploying drop tanks through the summer of 1943 had more to do with the muddle over requirement and confusion over production than with technical issues. Problems with local production in Britain led to a crash program in the United States, though the British plants came online in December 1943 in time for Operation *Argument*. In parallel, programs were under way in the spring of 1943 to increase the internal fuel capacity in the fighters. The P-47 required significant internal reconfiguration under the cockpit floor to increase tankage by 65 gallons, resulting in the P-47D-15 version, which increased its combat radius to 430 miles (690km). A further change on P-47-D-25 added another 65 gallons and this version began arriving in May 1944.

There were hopes that the P-38 would solve the long-range-escort requirement, but the aircraft suffered from engine-reliability issues at high altitudes and was a disappointment. These P-38Hs are from the 338th Fighter Squadron, 55th Fighter Group, preparing to escort B-17s of the 91st Bombardment Group on the December 12, 1943, mission to Bremen. (NARA)

Because of pressure from the Eighth Air Force after the Schweinfurt raids, VIII Fighter Command began to receive the first P-38 group in October and a second in December 1943 as well as the new P-47D. In the event the P-38 proved to be a disappointment in the escort role as it had engine-reliability issues when operating at high altitudes, and its combat performance against typical German fighters was mediocre.

The most satisfactory solution to the escort problem was the new North American P-51. The baseline P-51B already had an impressive combat radius of 475 miles (765km), which was further extended by additional internal storage as well as drop tanks. Hunter had preferred the P-47 for the escort-fighter mission, and as a result the P-51B had been allotted to the tactical-fighter squadrons of the incoming Ninth Air Force. With the autumn 1943 command changes and the new emphasis on the deep-escort mission, Kepner received Arnold's support to switch the P-51B squadrons to Eighth Air Force control. The first P-51B squadrons arrived in September 1943 and became operational on December 5, 1943. The P-51 proved to be the best escort fighter, not only because of its range but also because of its exceptional performance against both the FW-190 and Bf-109. The P-51B and C were gradually supplanted by the P-51D, which began arriving in May 1944; it became the definitive escort fighter. With two 75-gallon wing tanks the P-51 had a radius of about 650 miles (1,050km), enabling it to reach Berlin, and this could be extended to 850 miles (1,370km) with two 108-gallon tanks, enough to reach Vienna.

USAAF combat groups 1942–44

	October 1942	January 1943	April 1943	July 1943	October 1943	January 1944	April 1944	July 1944	October 1944
Heavy bomber, ETO	9	7	12	16	20	28	39	41	41
Heavy bomber, MTO	2	5	6	8	6	3	21	21	21
Bomber subtotal	11	12	18	24	26	31	60	62	62
Fighter, ETO*	9	3	3	7	11	19	32	33	33
Fighter, MTO*	3	12	13	14	14	14	13	13	12
Fighter subtotal	12	15	16	21	25	33	45	46	45

*"Fighter" includes all fighters, including those attached to tactical commands

Order of battle: USSTAF, February 1944

Eighth Air Force		
1st Bombardment Division	**Brampton Grange, Huntingdonshire**	
1st Combat Bombardment Wing	RAF Bassingbourn	91st, 381st, 398th, and 482nd (P) Bombardment Groups
40th Combat Bombardment Wing	RAF Thurleigh	92nd, 305th, and 306th Bombardment Groups
41st Combat Bombardment Wing	RAF Molesworth	303rd, 379th, 384th Bombardment Groups
94th Combat Bombardment Wing	RAF Polebrook	351st, 401st, and 457th Bombardment Groups
67th Fighter Wing	Walcot Hall	20th, 352nd, 359th, and 364th Fighter Groups
2nd Bombardment Division	**Ketteringham Hall, Norfolk**	
2nd Combat Bombardment Wing	RAF Hethel	389th, 445th, and 453rd Bombardment Groups
14th Combat Bombardment Wing	RAF Shipdham	392nd, 491st, and 492nd Bombardment Groups
20th Combat Bombardment Wing	RAF Hardwick	93rd, 446th, 448th, 489th Bombardment Groups
96th Combat Bombardment Wing	RAF Horsham	458th Bombardment Groups
65th Fighter Wing	Saffron Walden	4th, 56th, 355th, and 356th Fighter Groups
3nd Bombardment Division	**RAF Honington, Norfolk**	
4th Combat Bombardment Wing	RAF Bury St Edmunds	94th, 385th, 388th, and 447th Bombardment Groups
13th Combat Bombardment Wing	RAF Horham	95th, 100th, and 390th Bombardment Groups
45th Combat Bombardment Wing	RAF Snetterton Heath	96th, 388th, and 452nd Bombardment Groups
66th Fighter Wing	Sawston Hall	55th, 78th, 353rd, 357th, 358th, and 361st Fighter Groups
Fifteenth Air Force		
5th Bombardment Wing	Foggia	2nd, 97th, 99th, 301st, 463rd, and 483rd Bombardment Groups
47th Bombardment Wing	Manduria	98th, 376th, 449th, and 450th Bombardment Groups
304th Bombardment Wing	Cerignola	454th, 455th, 456th, and 459th Bombardment Groups
306th Fighter Wing	Foggia	1st, 14th, 31st, 52nd, 82nd, 325th, and 332nd Fighter Groups

OPPOSING PLANS

USAAF PLANS

USAAF doctrine considered the destruction of enemy industry by precision daytime bombing its most important mission, starting with AWPD/1 (Air War Plan Directive) of August 12, 1941. Early plans had four main objectives: the disruption of the German electric-power system, the disruption of German transportation, the destruction of German oil and fuel supplies, and undermining German morale by attacks on cities. The plan assumed that it would be necessary to neutralize the Luftwaffe by attacks on its bases as well as airframe, aircraft engine, and aluminum plants as a preliminary stage in its campaign against German industry.

During discussions with their RAF counterparts in 1942 the enormous difference in tactical approach between the USAAF and the RAF quickly became evident. The RAF had attempted to conduct daytime raids against German military targets in 1939–40, but the losses had been so catastrophic that the RAF had switched to night attacks. Until late 1943, RAF nighttime bombing was not precise enough to attack anything other than cities, and so the mission became the indirect attack on German war industries through "de-housing" a large portion of Germany's urban population. American

To accelerate the introduction of the new P-51B Mustang into the long-range-escort role, the 354th Fighter Group was borrowed from the newly arriving Ninth Air Force to support Eighth Air Force missions at the end of 1943. This P-51B from the 353rd Fighter Squadron, 354th Fighter Group, was displayed to crews of the 401st Bombardment Group at Deenethorpe on December 27, 1943, for familiarization with the new aircraft prior to a mission to Ludwigshaven three days later, as there were some fears that it could be mistaken for the German Bf 109. (NARA)

planners were opposed to adopting this tactic for the USAAF because of skepticism about its effectiveness. Some senior USAAF commanders were also reluctant to engage in such a campaign because of the fear that it would not be acceptable to US popular opinion, which could undermine political support for the enormous costs associated with the USAAF's large bomber force. It was unlikely that the USAAF could convince its more experienced RAF counterparts to change their approach, so the USAAF was content to leave the campaign against German civilian morale to RAF Bomber Command and concentrate on other objectives. The US Joint Chiefs of Staff were willing to support the substantial diversion of industrial and human resources to the USAAF bomber program only if it contributed in a substantial way to the eventual defeat of Germany. Army Ground Force (AGF) commanders were adamant that the Luftwaffe be crippled before an amphibious landing in France, and in August 1942 President Roosevelt requested a new directive to achieve "complete air ascendency over the enemy."

These developments culminated in AWPD/42, which re-emphasized the air campaign against the Luftwaffe as the critical prelude to the eventual attack on German war industry. This envisioned a 16-month campaign from the autumn of 1942 into 1944. This was refined by the USAAF Committee of Operations, which submitted its report to Gen. Arnold on March 8, 1943. AWPD/42 was strongly opposed by the US Navy, which recognized that the plan would require a disproportionate share of the procurement funding going to the USAAF in 1943. As a result, the USAAF had to justify its focus on strategic bombing not only against a very different British tactical approach, but also against Navy criticism, which sought more resources for the Pacific. Nevertheless, the Casablanca conference in January 1943 between Roosevelt and Churchill reaffirmed the "Germany first" approach and reiterated the need for a strategic-bombing campaign to weaken Germany before an amphibious invasion could be staged. The Combined Chiefs of Staff issued the Casablanca Directive (CCS 166/1/D), which explained the mission of the air campaign as "the progressive destruction and dislocation of the German military, industrial and economic system, and the undermining of the morale of the German people to a point where their capacity for armed resistance is fatally weakened."

German airframe-assembly plants, 1944

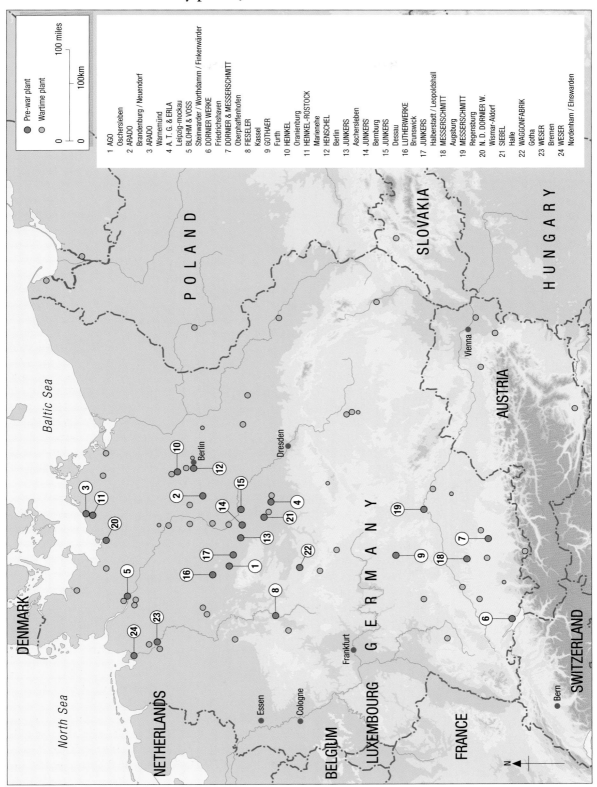

Pre-war plant
Wartime plant

100 miles
100km

1 AGO — Oschersleben
2 ARADO — Brandenburg / Neuendorf
3 ARADO — Warnemünd
4 A. T. G. & ERLA — Leipzig-mockau
5 BLOHM & VOSS — Steinwarder / Worthdamm / Finkenwärder
6 DORNIER WERKE — Friedrichshaven
7 DORNIER & MESSERSCHMITT — Oberpfaffenhofen
8 FIESELER — Kassel
9 GOTHAER — Furth
10 HEINKEL — Oranienburg
11 HEINKEL-ROSTOCK — Marienehe
12 HENSCHEL — Berlin
13 JUNKERS — Aschersleben
14 JUNKERS — Bernburg
15 JUNKERS — Dessau
16 LUTHERWERKE — Brunswick
17 JUNKERS — Halberstadt / Leopoldshall
18 MESSERSCHMITT — Augsburg
19 MESSERSCHMITT — Regensburg
20 N. D. DORNIER W. — Wismar-Aldorf
21 SIEBEL — Halle
22 WAGGONFABRIK — Gotha
23 WESER — Bremen
24 WESER — Nordenham / Einswarden

Baltic Sea

North Sea

POLAND

SLOVAKIA

HUNGARY

AUSTRIA

Vienna

Berlin

Dresden

G E R M A N Y

Frankfurt

Essen

Cologne

Bern

DENMARK

NETHERLANDS

BELGIUM

LUXEMBOURG

FRANCE

SWITZERLAND

N

A critical ingredient in the escort-fighter dilemma was the production of pressurized drop tanks suitable for use at high altitudes. This P-51D of the 361st Fighter Group is seen with two of the standard 75 - gallon tanks below its wings. (NARA)

In response to the Casablanca Directive, the RAF and USAAF drew up plans for the Combined Bomber Offensive in April 1943, which were formally released on June 10, 1943. The RAF bomber commanders dubbed this the "Eaker Plan." The Combined Bomber Offensive categorized the objectives as "intermediate," "primary," and "secondary." The attack on the Luftwaffe fighter force was designated as an intermediate objective, since it was necessary prior to the prosecution of the main campaign. The primary targets remained German submarine facilities, the aircraft industry other than fighters, ball-bearing plants, and the oil and fuel systems; secondary objectives were the synthetic rubber industry and German motor transport industry. The Combined Bomber Offensive was a fig leaf disguising the fundamental disagreement between USAAF and RAF staffs over the conduct of the air war, and tacitly accepted that the RAF would continue with its own approach of the nighttime bombing of German cities while the USAAF conducted a separate daytime campaign. To deal with the Luftwaffe the RAF preferred an expansion of Operations *Rhubarb* and *Circus*, which were fighter and light-bomber sweeps against German fighter bases in France and the Low Countries. This did not directly impact the Combined Bomber Offensive since these missions were conducted by the RAF's Second Tactical Air Force and later by the USAAF's Ninth Air Force.

When the Combined Bomber Offensive plan was approved by the Combined Chiefs of Staff in May 1943 it also received the codename *Pointblank*. This codename took on different meanings for the RAF and USAAF, with the RAF using it to describe the entire Combined Bomber Offensive effort while the USAAF generally used it to refer to the anti-Luftwaffe mission. Operation *Pointblank* was reaffirmed at the Quebec conference in August 1943, when the date for the *Overlord* invasion was initially set as May 1, 1944. The Combined Bomber Offensive plan also assigned a high priority to attacking of the German U-boat force, including both the yards in Germany and the bases in France on the Sea of Biscay. In the event this target diminished in priority by the end of 1943 as Battle of the Atlantic swung in favor of the Allies.

As described in "The Strategic Situation" earlier in this book, the operations from August 1942 to October 1943 unfolded much less satisfactorily than the USAAF had expected. The "self-defending bomber" concept proved unsustainable in the face of Luftwaffe improvements, and a substantial long-range escort-fighter force was necessary for the survival of the daytime bomber campaign. The USAAF quickly adapted under difficult circumstances, but the changes as well as winter weather postponed the final phase of Operation *Pointblank*, codenamed Operation *Argument*, from November 1943 to February 1944.

The tactical aim of Operation *Argument* was to affect the Luftwaffe's "production-wastage differential." What this jargon meant was that the campaign had to suppress German fighter production as well as increase Luftwaffe fighter losses (wastage) in order to shrink the size of the German fighter force. This was a classic attrition strategy. With Allied intelligence raising growing doubts about the reliability of bomber-gunner claims against German fighters, USAAF commanders sought other approaches to increasing the Luftwaffe's fighter attrition. General Arnold's 1944 new year's message to the Eighth and Fifteenth Air Force commanders concluded with the admonition: "This is a MUST – Destroy the Enemy Air Force wherever you find them, in the air, on the ground, and in the factories." While this might seem like a routine pep talk, it addressed one of the key tactical dilemmas facing the expanding deep-escort-fighter force. Should the fighters be confined to "close-escort" of the bombers, staying near the combat boxes and not pursuing the German fighters? Or should they be given free rein to chase down the fighters, even if it meant leaving the immediate vicinity of the bombers? Major-General William Kepner, commander of VIII Fighter Command, had been urging a more aggressive policy, a point of view apparently sanctioned by Arnold's letter. When Doolittle visited Kepner's headquarters in early January 1944, he noticed a sign on the office wall that read: "The first duty of the Eighth Air Force fighters is to bring the bombers back alive." Kepner explained that the sign dated back to Hunter's days in command. Doolittle ordered the sign to be replaced with a new one reading: "The first duty of the Eighth Air Force fighters is to destroy German fighters." Doolittle amplified his intent by instructing Kepner that "We'll still provide a reasonable fighter escort for the bombers, but the bulk of your fighters will go hunting for Jerries. Flush them out in the air and beat them up on the ground on the way home. Your first priority is to take the offensive." Doolittle's January directives fundamentally changed the dynamics of fighter combat during Operation *Argument* and had a decisive impact on its outcome.

GERMAN PLANS

The year 1943 was the turning point in the war for Germany, with the loss of the strategic initiative on the Russian front after the defeat of the Kursk offensive in the summer, the defeat of the Atlantic U-boat campaign, and the escalation of Allied bombing attacks. In the case of the bomber threat, it should be recalled that Allied attacks up to the end of 1943 only accounted for about 16 percent of the total tonnage dropped on Germany during the war, a mere foretaste of the cataclysm to come. Allied bomber attacks were all very worrisome, but by the autumn and early winter of 1943 it seemed to many German leaders that the Luftwaffe fighter force, in conjunction with the flak arm, had stalemated the Allied campaigns. The heavy RAF losses during the Berlin raids in the autumn of 1943 and the USAAF losses over Schweinfurt in October 1943 led the future Luftwaffe chief of staff, Generalleutnant Karl Koller, to believe that the Luftwaffe could inflict 30-percent losses on the Allied bombers in 1944, a level of loss that would probably stop the bombing raids.

The threat of USAAF bomber attacks against the Luftwaffe fighter industry led to a program to disperse assembly facilities to smaller and better-concealed locations. This is an Fw 190 assembly facility created in a tunnel near Gevelsberg in the forested hills east of Düsseldorf. (NARA)

In response to Hitler's boast of "Fortress Europe," in September 1943 President Franklin Roosevelt derided it as a "fortress without a roof." The Luftwaffe's main task at the end of 1943 was to create such a roof. The short-term solution of redeploying fighter units from other fronts to the defense of the Reich was not enough and the long-term solution was to create additional fighter and flak units for Reich defense. There was no consensus among senior German leaders regarding priorities for the production of new weapons, with

flak, fighter, and bomber factions all vying for a larger fraction of the industrial output. Hitler, Göring, and Jeschonnek all favored retaliation over defense, and so favored an expanded bomber effort at the expense of fighter expansion. Even the Luftwaffe fighter advocates argued amongst themselves whether the priority should go to night fighters to deal with the RAF nighttime attacks, or day fighters to deal with the USAAF daytime attacks.

The expansion of the fighter force in 1943–44 was slowed by Hitler's preference for offensive solutions. Paradoxically, he remained a strong supporter of the flak arm, largely for domestic political reasons. Civilians in bombed-out cities were angry over the apparent ineffectiveness of the Luftwaffe fighter force since the aerial combat took place far outside their view; on the other hand, the rattle of the nearby flak batteries provided assurance that some defense against the dreaded bombers was under way. In the case of aircraft production, Hitler resisted Milch's attempt in the summer of 1943 to expand fighter production at the expense of bomber production. As a result of the July RAF raids on the Ruhr and the USAAF raids on Schweinfurt, Milch unveiled Program 224 on October 1, 1943, nicknamed the "Reich defense program," which marked a shift in emphasis to fighter production. The program increased the production goal for single-engine fighters to 4,150 and of twin-engine fighters to 1,750, but kept the number of bombers and attack aircraft relatively stable. This did not meet with Hitler's approval, and, under the December 1943 Program 225, Milch was obliged to cut back on fighter-production goals to 2,933 fighters a month in order to free up resources for the manufacture of the He-177 bomber that Hitler wanted for the revived "mini-Blitz" campaign against Britain, Operation Steinbock. These attacks would be amplified by the use of radical new weapons, especially the Luftwaffe's new Fi-103 (V-1) cruise missile and the army's A-4 (V-2) ballistic missile. Enormous resources were thrown away on the A-4 missile program.

To some extent, the controversy over industrial allocations were temporarily ignored because of promises from the Reich's armament minister, Albert Speer, that it would be possible to substantially expand all aircraft production in 1944 through increased efficiency, greater standardization, and the diversion of more resources out of the civilian economy. Even in 1943, Germany had still not converted as much of its civilian production into military production as had Britain, America, or Russia, and this industrial reserve would prove to be an enormous resource throughout 1944 in spite of American attacks on the German aircraft industry. Throughout 1943 most German aircraft plants were working a single-shift, 40-hour working week. Speer's efforts to increase the efficiency of the aircraft industry led to a general increase in fighter production through the first half of 1944 regardless of priorities.

German fighter production by quarter, 1943–44

	I/1943	II	III	IV	Total 1943	I/1944	II	III	IV	Total 1944
Me-109	1,185	1,771	1,894	1,568	6,418	2,451	3,301	4,328	4,132	14,212
Fw-190	740	823	923	722	3,208	1,257	2,475	4,049	3,630	11,411
All twin-engine fighters	407	489	653	563	2,112	589	822	832	663	2,906
Total	2,332	3,083	3,470	2,853	11,738	4,297	6,598	9,209	8,425	28,529

OPERATION *POINTBLANK*

PRELUDE TO OPERATION *ARGUMENT*

By December 1943, Operation *Pointblank* was three months behind its timetable to support the *Overlord* invasion plan. As of November 1943 the Eighth Air Force had only about 65 percent of its planned force available, about 22 of the planned 32 bomber groups, because of the continued diversion of units to the Mediterranean theater to support operations on Sicily in July 1943, and in Italy starting in September 1943. Nevertheless, the Italian campaign had unexpected benefits for the bomber campaign when Allied advances in Italy permitted the deployment of the Fifteenth Air Force to bases around Foggia in November 1943, enabling attacks into southern Germany, Austria, Hungary, and Romania. The contribution of this new heavy-bomber force was postponed because of its commitment in support of the Anzio landings in January 1944, yet another reason for the delay of the culminating phase of *Pointblank*.

The delay in the start of Operation *Argument* was frustrating for Allied commanders, but ultimately it benefited the conduct of the campaign. The number of heavy-bomber groups and escort-fighter groups substantially increased at the end of 1943. From November 1943, when *Argument* was originally scheduled to begin, the Eighth Air Force had 22 heavy-bomber groups, but by February 1944, when it actually began, this had more than doubled to 48 bomber groups in both Eighth and Fifteenth Air Forces. Likewise, escort-fighter strength increased from 12 fighter groups in the Eighth Air Force in November 1943 to 21 in February 1944. Besides the quantitative improvement, there was substantial qualitative improvement. A larger number of Pathfinder bombers were available in February, so more attacks could be conducted in overcast winter weather. The escort-fighter force had made a dramatic improvement because of wider availability of drop tanks for the P-47 fighter, and the first groups of the new P-51 Mustang fighter were operational. Besides the immediate improvements in the Eighth and Fifteenth Air Forces, the US Army had also deployed the new Ninth Air Force to Britain to serve as the tactical air force for the Normandy invasion. In the meantime, its medium bombers were committed against targets in France, freeing up the heavy bombers to concentrate on their *Pointblank* missions.

While some of the early postponements of Operation *Argument* were because of bomber strength and fighter-escort issues, the predominant issue in December 1943 and January 1944 was the weather. Typical early winter

weather either 'socked in' the departure bases in Britain, or obscured the targets in Germany. The operation needed relatively clear conditions in both locations. Although the *Argument* attacks were postponed, bombing operations continued through these months. These alternate missions served a variety of purposes, including efforts to test and improve all-weather bombing tactics using the new H2X radar and associated Pathfinder aircraft. In addition, there was a general consensus among senior USAAF commanders that the missions contributed to the overall goal of wearing down the Luftwaffe through attrition. The targets tended to be along the North Sea coast since the coastline could be targeted using the H2X radar. Nevertheless, it was evident that the new radar-techniques were not especially accurate, and that a serious effort against the fighter factories would require clear weather. The early winter also saw a steady growth in the size of the missions, reaching the 600-bomber mark by the end of November and the 700 mark by mid-December 1943.

When the weather cleared briefly on January 11, 1944, the Eighth Air Force decided to launch a major attack against the Fw-190 plant at Oschersleben. A total of 663 B-17 and B-24 bombers from all three bombardment divisions were dispatched and escort fighters were provided for the entire distance, though with very thin coverage over the target area by the only available P-51 group. The mission was disrupted by the changing weather, which led to the recall of most of the bombers; only 238 bombers attacked their targets and of these only 139 at Oschersleben. The attack stirred up a hornet's nest on the Luftwaffe side because of fear that the formations were heading for Berlin. Escorts or not, the Luftwaffe fighters began attacking the bomber streams, starting over the Zuiderzee in the Netherlands and continuing through the bombing runs. The air battles were the first for the new Sturmstaffel 1, a unit with heavily armored Fw-190A-8s designed for close-assault tactics against the bombers. Even single-engine fighters earmarked for night-fighting were thrown into the fray that day. Bomber losses were heavy, with 60 lost over Germany, equivalent to the bloody Schweinfurt missions in 1943, and five more scrapped because of

LEFT
Black Tuesday, the ill-fated mission of January 11, 1944, was disrupted by the winter weather. This is a B-17 of the 390th Bombardment Group, 3rd Bombardment Division, on its way to attack the aircraft plants around Brunswick. (NARA)

RIGHT
While waiting for the weather to clear, the Eighth Air Force attacked targets in France. This B-17 of the 100th Bombardment Group suffered a direct flak hit to the rear gun station during a mission near Dieppe against V-weapon sites on January 21, 1944. (NARA)

Escorting the bombers: Mission 182, Oschersleben and Halberstadt, January 11, 1944

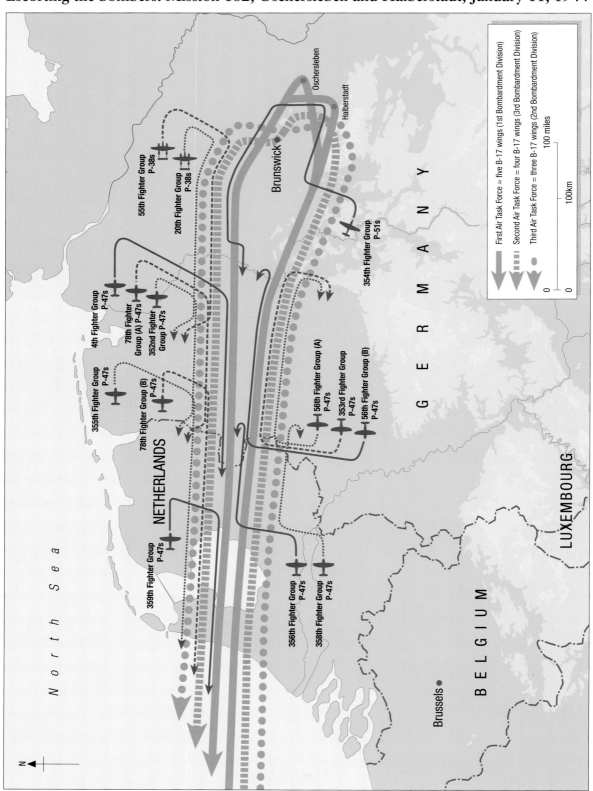

First Air Task Force = five B-17 wings (1st Bombardment Division)
Second Air Task Force = four B-17 wings (3rd Bombardment Division)
Third Air Task Force = three B-17 wings (2nd Bombardment Division)

100 miles
100km

Oschersleben
Halberstadt
Brunswick

GERMANY

354th Fighter Group
P-51s

55th Fighter Group
P-38s

20th Fighter Group
P-38s

4th Fighter Group
P-47s

78th Fighter
Group (A) P-47s

352nd Fighter
Group P-47s

355th Fighter Group
P-47s

78th Fighter Group (B)
P-47s

56th Fighter Group (A)
P-47s

353rd Fighter Group
P-47s

56th Fighter Group (B)
P-47s

NETHERLANDS

359th Fighter Group
P-47s

356th Fighter
Group P-47s

358th Fighter Group
P-47s

North Sea

BELGIUM

LUXEMBOURG

Brussels

N

extensive damage after returning to England. Luftwaffe losses were also high, with 53 aircraft shot down and 31 damaged beyond economical repair, but I Jagdkorps' commander, Josef "Beppo" Schmid, regarded "Black Tuesday" as "the last victory of the Luftwaffe against the US air force." What was different about the January 11 mission was the exceptionally heavy losses inflicted by the USAAF escort fighters on the Luftwaffe, with the various fighter squadrons claiming 31 confirmed and 12 probable kills. The January 11 mission was a sharp reminder of the limits of daytime bombing in harsh winter weather, and convinced Doolittle to delay the initiation of Operation *Argument* until a period of clear weather.

Missions over Germany for the rest of January were few, because of continued poor winter weather. The January fighting was indecisive for both sides, but as a battle of attrition the tide was turning. German losses had been 233 fighters during 4,049 sorties, which was a loss rate of 5 percent; the USAAF loss rate was half that. The Reich defense force was still starving for new pilots while the Eighth Air Force continued to grow. The Fifteenth Air Force continued to play a negligible role in the battle over Germany since it was tied down supporting the amphibious landing at Anzio near Rome.

January saw the continued refinement of tactics on both sides. "Beppo" Schmid continued to press his units to group up into large formations prior to conducting an assault against the bombers. This was an echo of the RAF's "Big Wing" arguments during the Battle of Britain. Schmid argued that the massed formations had a much better chance of success against the bomber boxes than pinprick strikes by small units. Procedures were put in place to form the groups over eastern Holland, northwest Germany, and the corridor between Bremen and Hannover.

The first display of the new and more aggressive American fighter tactics based on Doolittle's directive took place on January 24. The 356th Fighter Group chased down a gaggle of 15 German fighters for 65 miles (105km) before downing six of them, and one flight chased eight of them down to treetop level, downing three. Previously there had been a prohibition against US fighters descending below 18,000ft (5,490m). The new policy was not without its critics, because of the potential effect on the morale of the bomber crews, and even Spaatz questioned its soundness. In spite of the new American tactics, Göring continued to insist that the fighters avoid the American escort fighters and concentrate on the bombers, accusing the pilots of cowardice in fearing to attack the heavily armed bombers. "Beppo" Schmid later complained that Göring's instructions had disastrous consequences for his fighters: "Knowing that they need not fear an attack by the German fighter aircraft, American fighters are able to move into range and attack the German fighters from above." Adolf Galland later stated that as a consequence of Göring's directive, the Luftwaffe lost the air war.

This map shows the fighter escort relay system used on typical bombing missions. This map shows the initial plan for the mission; weather conditions interfered with its actual execution. Within each task force the bomb wings flew about 9 miles (14km) from each other; between the task forces the separation was 72 miles (116km). Because of the speed differential between the fighters and bombers, the fighter groups had to weave in their defensive zone to keep pace with the bombers. The missions included 291 B-17s from the 1st Bombardment Division, 138 B-24s from the 2nd Bombardment Division, and 234 B-17s from the 3rd Bombardment Division. Each fighter group averaged 48 fighters, so there were about 670 fighters on each escort mission; 592 were actually dispatched on this mission. Coverage was heaviest on the return flight, on the presumption that there would be more damaged bombers and stragglers. The mission was also noteworthy for the award of the Medal of Honor to Colonel James Howard, 354th Fighter Group, for single-handedly defending a B-17 wing from attack from more than 30 enemy aircraft.

The Fifteenth Air Force's commitments in Italy limited its support of Operation *Argument*. However, extensive strikes were conducted against Luftwaffe fighter bases in the Po Valley, knocking out many aircraft such as this Bf 109G at Campo Formido airfield. (NARA)

The USSTAF wanted a week of decent weather in which to launch Operation *Argument* against 12 selected aircraft-assembly and aircraft sub-component plants. The weather in early February was no better than it was in January, and there were only a few missions to the usual targets along the western German border at Wilhelmshaven, Frankfurt, and Brunswick. The February 10 mission to the fighter plants near Brunswick was further evidence of the impact Doolittle's January fighter directive was having. Only the 3rd Bombardment Division participated with 169 B-17s, but 466 fighters were dispatched. The weather in Germany was adequate enough for I Jagdkorps to get 303 fighters in the air and to build up a number of large attack formations. Air battles broke out over a wide area with heavy losses on both sides. Schmid's fighters claimed 43 bombers plus 5 probable kills; US records indicate 30 lost and missing. However, I Jagdkorps fighter losses had been heavy, with 30 aircraft shot down and 16 more damaged beyond repair; the USAAF reported 11 fighters lost. A repeat attack against the Frankfurt area the following day by 212 B-17s and 606 fighters encountered less opposition, because of the poor weather. A total of only 187 Luftwaffe fighters took off, but only about 70 were able to intercept the American force. They claimed three bombers and ten fighters at a cost of 12 aircraft lost and five too damaged to repair.

The first hints that the weather might finally cooperate occurred during the third week of February. Allied intelligence had been regularly deciphering weather forecasts issued by an SS weather station based in Krakow, since the Germans had better weather forecasting on the Russian Front. On February 19 information from this station suggested that a windy, high-pressure front in the Baltic would move southwest toward Germany and might provide a week of cold, clear weather. Spaatz's operations officer, Fred Anderson, began pressing for the launch of Operation *Argument*. Fifteenth Air Force participation, at least for the first few days, was in doubt because of the demands of supporting the Anzio front. Regardless, the orders were passed down to Eighth Air Force that on February 20, 1944, Mission 226 would kick off Operation *Argument*; this was what would eventually be called "Big Week."

OPERATION *ARGUMENT*

Operation *Argument* had 12 principal targets, all of which were major aircraft-assembly plants. The attack on February 20 was aimed at three clusters of these around Leipzig, Gotha, and Brunswick. The attack was aided by an RAF mission the night before against Leipzig, which helped exhaust the supply of flak ammunition in that area. The 3rd Bombardment Division dispatched 314 B-17s to hit the Tutow plants in northeast Germany, while the 1st and 2nd Bombardment Divisions sent out 417 B-17s and 272 B-24s to attack the plants in the Brunswick/Leipzig corridor. Fighter escorts totaled 835 aircraft, including 73 of the new P-51B fighters, but mainly comprised P-47 Thunderbolts. To further disrupt Luftwaffe fighter defenses, the heavy-bomber force was preceded by two spoiling attacks by medium bombers of the Ninth Air Force against scattered targets along the Dutch coast.

The Luftwaffe response was poorly coordinated and many units of Luftflotte 3 failed to intercept the incoming force. The 1. Jagddivision was assigned to deal with the 3rd Bombardment Division attack toward Tutow, while the 2. and 3. Jagddivisionen were assigned to attack the main force. I Jagdkorps failed to group together any large attack formations and the fighters attacked in a disjointed fashion. Of the 362 Luftwaffe fighters taking off, only 155 managed to reach the US force. The Luftwaffe claimed 27 bombers and 8 fighters against US reports of 26 bombers and 6 fighters lost or missing. However, German losses were high, totaling 28 fighters lost and 21 aircraft damaged beyond repair in I Jagdkorps alone, plus additional losses in the forward-deployed units of Luftflotte 3. The 1. Jagdkorps losses amounted to nearly a third of the force that had taken part in combat. Expecting to encounter a major German response, the US bomber crews were relieved at the modest defense on February 20. Bombing was generally good at the sites where visible aiming was possible, and the Ju-88 plants in the Leipzig area and the Bf-109 plant at Erla suffered significant damage, including an estimated 40 fighters destroyed on the ground at the Erla plant.

Operation *Argument* resumed on February 21, with the RAF Bomber Command preceding the assault with a night attack on Stuttgart. The Eighth Air Force dispatched 861 bombers and 679 fighters against a variety of aircraft plants in the Diepholz–Achmer area. The Luftwaffe response was hampered by poor weather and only 282 fighters were launched. I Jagdkorps

BELOW, LEFT
A maintenance crew from the 323rd Squadron, 91st Bombardment Group, prepare "Miss Ouachita" for a mission at their base at Bassingbourne. Piloted by Lieutenant Spencer Osterberg, it was lost on a mission against German aircraft factories on February 21, 1944. It was shot down near Hanover by an Fw 190 piloted by the well-known ace, Heinz Bär of 6./Jagdgeschwader 1, his 184th kill to date. (NARA)

BELOW, RIGHT
B-17F and B-17G bombers of the 385th Bombardment Group, 3rd Bombardment Group, on their way to attack aircraft plants in the Rostock area on February 24, 1944, during Big Week. (NARA)

1 **First Air Task Force (1st Bombardment Division; 291 B-17)**
Oschersleben Force: 91st, 92nd, 303rd, 351st, 379th, 381th, and 401st Bombardment Groups
Halberstadt Force: 305th, 306th, 384th, and 482nd Bombardment Groups

1A 356th Fighter Group (48 P-47s)
1B 56th Fighter Group (37 P-47s)
1C 354th Fighter Group (49 P-51s)
1D 4th Fighter Group (49 P-47s)
1E 359th Fighter Group (61 P-47s)

2 **Second Air Task Force (3rd Bombardment Division; 269 B-17s)**
94th, 95th, 96th, 100th, 385th, 388th, 390th, 447th Bombardment Groups

2A 353rd Fighter Group (58 P-47)
2B 55th Fighter Group (54 P-38)
(78th Fighter Group mission aborted because of weather)

3 **Third Air Task Force (2nd Bombardment Division; 165 B-24s)**
44th, 93rd, 389th, 392nd, 445th, 446th, and 448th Bombardment Groups

3A 358th Fighter Group (47 P-47s)
3B 56th Fighter Group (36 P-47s)
(20th and 356th Fighter Group missions were cancelled or aborted in flight because of weather)

▼ EVENTS

1 Bombers begin forming up over England at 0950hrs GMT. Initial formations of the 1st Bombardment Division depart the English coast around 1012hrs; 3rd Bombardment Division at 1023hrs; 2nd Bombardment Division at 1032hrs.

2 Luftwaffe Seeräuber signals-intelligence station at Zeist reports first activity of American bombers at 0828hrs. Fighter units in France, the Netherlands, Belgium, Germany, and Denmark are alerted.

3 Bomber stream enters Dutch airspace around 1034hrs, with escort fighters joining shortly after over Zuiderzee; German fighters are told to mass on the German–Dutch border to minimize fighter contact. The 1. Jagddivision is committed to Brunswick, 2. Jagddivision to Hannover and Paderborn, and 3. Jagddivision to Bremen and Bielefeld.

4 First heavy contact between German fighters and the bomber stream begins around 1053hrs over Linden; German fighter strength is estimated at over 50 fighters. The German fighters are engaged by the escorting 56th Fighter Group. While initial air battles begin, at 1104hrs German controllers tell other formations to begin to mass 15 miles (25km) northwest of Hannover.

5 Fighting between German fighters and the American bombers and escorts had generally shifted to the Osnabruck area by 1140hrs. I Jagdkorps puts up 239 sorties, with 207 making contact. The 3. Jagddivision units that make a second sortie are ordered to the Münster area.

6 Weather over England has turned so bad that Doolittle orders a recall order at 1145hrs. The recall order is not passed to lead elements of 1st Air Task Force since they are so near their targets. Elements of 2nd and 3rd Air Task Forces begin to turn back home.

7 1st Combat Wing (91st and 381st Bombardment Groups) begins its bombing attack over Oschersleben at 1147hrs; 41st Combat Wing (303rd and 379th Bombardment Groups) attacks at 1149hrs; and 94th Combat Wing (351st and 401st Bombardment Groups) attacks at 1152hrs. The 91st, 381st, and 398th Bombardment Groups later receive the Presidential Unit Citation for actions that day.

8 The 354th Fighter Group commander, Major James Howard, becomes separated from his flight while shooting down a Bf-110. On returning to the bomber stream he finds it unprotected and so begins to single-handedly rebuff numerous German fighter attacks over the course of 30 minutes, shooting down two more fighters. The bomber crews are so impressed with his action that he is later awarded the Medal of Honor, the only USAAF fighter pilot to win this distinction in the ETO.

9 The 40th Combat Wing (92nd and 306th Bombardment Groups) bombs Halberstadt starting at 1154hrs, followed by the 40–41 Composite Wing (305th and 384th Bombardment Groups).

10 While on the way, the 14th Combat Wing spots an opening in the clouds around 1155hrs and attacks a target of opportunity, the rail yard at Meppen.

11 Lead elements of 2nd Air Task Force, starting with the 94th Bombardment Group, drop bombs on secondary targets, starting with the Waggum plant outside Brunswick. At 1228hrs German controllers instruct all aircraft still airborne to mass over Osnabruck.

12 Flying out of France, I/Jagdgeschwader 26 begins to intercept a returning bomber stream over the Netherlands and is vectored north over the Zuiderzee to intercept the 306th Bombardment Group around 1300hrs, which is off course because of the weather and over the Nordhorn. Eight of 19 bombers are claimed, but three crash-land in England.

13 At 1342hrs German controllers order all fighters not in contact to land. Claims for the day are 113 American aircraft. By division, these claims are (bomber + fighter): 1. Jagddivision (17 + 3); 2. Jagddivision (54 + 1); 3. Jagddivision (34 + 4). The high scores for the day are Jagdgeschwader 1 and Jagdgeschwader 11, both with 22 claims. Total German losses are 53 aircraft shot down and 31 damaged beyond repair.

14 The first US bombers arrive over the English coast at 1346hrs. Total losses on the mission were 60 bombers and 5 fighters shot down; five more bombers were scrapped in England because of heavy damage.

PRELUDE TO OPERATION *ARGUMENT*: BLACK TUESDAY OVER OSCHERSLEBEN, JANUARY 11, 1944

Winter weather continues to delay the start of the full-scale attack on the German fighter industry

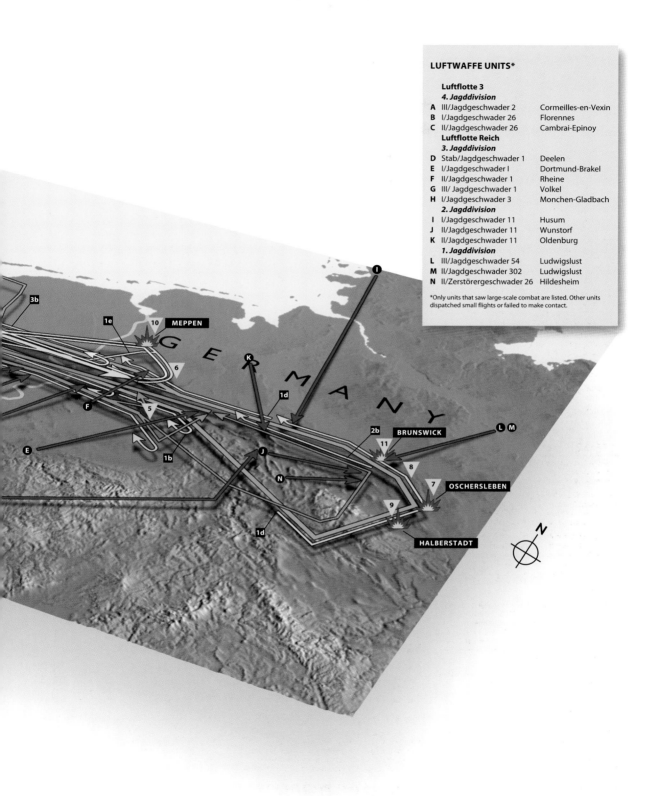

GERMANY

3b

1e   10   MEPPEN

6

K

1d

F

5

2b   BRUNSWICK
11

E

L   M

1b

J

8

N

7   OSCHERSLEBEN

9

1d

HALBERSTADT

I

N

claimed 20 bombers and seven fighters, and actual US losses were 23 bombers and 8 fighters, some because of poor weather and some lost to Luftflotte 3 attacks. The losses suffered by I Jagdkorps were again heavy, with 11 aircraft shot down and 14 damaged beyond repair.

On the third day of Big Week, February 22, Eighth Air Force put up 799 bombers and 659 fighters, but weather over England forced the 3rd Bombardment Division to abort their mission to Schweinfurt, and ultimately only 255 bombers reached the target area around Oschersleben and Bernberg. This was the first mission where the Fifteenth Air Force was finally able to participate, operating from bases in Italy, sending 183 bombers toward Regensberg. In contrast to the two previous days, the weather conditions were good enough that I Jagdkorps was finally able to get its planes airborne in time to build up large attack formations, and they also took advantage of a gap in escort coverage, hitting the bombers hard. A total of 332 fighters took part, claiming 55 bombers and 11 fighters against actual total losses of 45 bombers and 12 fighters to all causes. The I Jagdkorps losses were 11 aircraft shot down and 16 damaged beyond repair. The autonomous 7. Jagddivision in the south shot down 14 bombers from Fifteenth Air Force.

Poor weather on February 23 gave the Eighth Air Force a respite, but Fifteenth Air Force attacked from Italy with 102 bombers against ball-bearing plants in Steyr, Austria. The next Eighth Air Force attack on February 24 was against the dreaded Schweinfurt area. Once again, the 3rd Bombardment Division staged a separate attack toward Rostock in northeast Germany while the 1st and 2nd Divisions struck the primary targets at Schweinfurt and Gotha. The Fifteenth Air Force returned to Steyr; in all some 923 bombers set off on the various missions. The German fighter response was intense and included a significant number of night fighters, totaling 336 fighters.

The campaign against the aircraft plants was eventually extended to the aero-engine industry. This is the Henschel aircraft-engine plant in Altenbaum near Kassel. The Bf-109 in the foreground was used for engine testing. These test aircraft were often used for factory defense as well. (NARA)

Doolittle's decision to free the escort fighters from close escort increased attrition against German fighters. This dramatic gun-camera footage is from the P-51B flown by Lieutenant-Colonel Glenn Duncan of the 353rd Fighter Group on the mission of February 22, 1944. After strafing a German airfield, Duncan caught this Fw 190 alone and unaware. Hits on the right wing root caused the landing gear to drop; the aircraft crashed shortly after. Duncan was credited with 19.5 kills during 1944. (NARA)

The I Jagdkorps claimed 52 bombers and 7 fighters against actual Eighth Air Force total losses of 46 bombers and 10 fighters from all causes. To amplify the damage, RAF Bomber Command struck Schweinfurt that night. The October 1943 attack had already led to extensive damage to the ball-bearing plants and an effort to disperse the industry in the wake of the attack left fewer valuable targets; the February 24 attack was a *coup de grâce*. A far more significant result of the February 24 attack was the heavy destruction at the Gotha aircraft plant.

The attacks on February 25 were aimed primarily at southern Germany, with 754 bombers and 899 fighters from the Eighth Air Force and 176 bombers from the Fifteenth Air Force. A diversionary force was sent out toward the North Sea in hopes of distracting German fighters, and as a result both the 1. and 2. Jagddivisionen were alerted but not dispatched on intercept. Because of the distraction, I Jagdkorps put up only 100 fighters that day and the 3. Jagddivision claimed six bombers for a loss of five fighters destroyed and one damaged beyond repair. Most of Eighth Air Force's losses that day were from flak rather than fighters, with a total of 34 bombers lost to all causes. It was an especially successful mission from the bombing standpoint, causing extensive damage at the Regensburg and Augsburg plants. The 7. Jagddivision intercepted the much smaller Fifteenth Air Force formations, which lost 33 bombers.

The weather on February 26 again turned bad, ending the Big Week surge for the time being. In the week of attacks, the Eighth and Fifteenth Air Forces had conducted about 3,800 bomber sorties and dropped 10,000 tons of bombs. Bomber losses were lighter than anticipated, at 226 B-17s and B-24s, or about 6 percent; fighter sorties had totaled 3,673 with 28 losses, and total US aircrew losses were about 2,600 killed, missing, and captured. I Jagdkorps had never managed to seriously contest the attacks on the scale that they had accomplished in 1943, largely because of the presence of the USAAF escort fighters as well as the complications imposed by the winter weather. There had been only 1,412 Luftwaffe sorties, and losses had totaled 145 aircraft with 122 crew killed and 44 wounded – a loss rate of about 10 percent. Other units, including the

BIG WEEK: BATTLE ALONG THE "BOMBER AUTOBAHN," FEBRUARY 20, 1944

The start of Big Week saw frequent air battles between the bomber streams and Reich defense forces, and the 91st Bombardment Group reported that, "enemy opposition was stronger than it had been for the past three weeks." The B-17s of the 91st Bombardment Group, identified by the large "A" in a white triangle on their tail (1), were assigned targets in the Leipzig–Aschersleben area, but were diverted by their Pathfinders to Oschersleben because of cloud cover over Aschersleben. The group dispatched 40 B-17 bombers, which formed up into two combat boxes, A and B. One of the boxes was hit by a formation of four Fw-190 fighters (2), which "made a very vigorous attack on this formation," according to the 401st Squadron debriefing. The 322nd Squadron made one claim, a Bf-109, but one bomber was lost and at least one seriously damaged. The precise identity of the attacking German formation is not known, but it was most likely from 3. Jagddivision units such as Jagdgeschwader 1 and Jagdgeschwader 11.

The B-17G (3) has the Bendix chin turret in the nose (4), a Sperry A-1 dorsal turret (5), and a Sperry Type A-2 ball turret in the belly (6), each armed with twin Browning M2 .50-cal aircraft machine guns. This version of the machine gun had a higher rate of fire than the ground version, about 800 rounds per minute compared with 500. There was an enormous gas blast from these weapons since they expended about 15 rounds per second, or about half a pound of propellant per second. The Bendix turret carried 365 rounds of ammunition for each gun and ejected the spent cases through chutes at the bottom (7). The Bendix turret was operated by the gunner above using a controller yoke and a flip-down N-6 gunsight that was synchronized with the motion of the guns.

The FW-190A-8 had a pair of 20mm MG 151s in the wing root (8) and a pair of the more powerful 30mm MK 108s in the wing (9). Allied intelligence estimated that the 20mm round had a 6 percent probability of inflicting a kill on a heavy bomber, but that the 30mm round, because of its larger high-explosive fill, had a 25 percent probability. The FW-190A-8 also had a pair of MG 131 13mm machine guns in the nose in front of the canopy, but these were often deleted and faired over as the pilots thought that they added too much weight for too little destructive power against bombers. There were a number of other Rüsatz armament packages for the FW-190A-8, including different mixtures of internal and external cannon.

7. Jagddivision in southern Germany and elements of Luftflotte 3 in France and the Netherlands, had also taken part in the fighting but on a smaller scale. For example, the "Abbeville Boys," Jagdgeschwader 26 of Luftflotte 3, had seen considerable action on both February 24 and 25 and had claimed 32 bombers and eight fighters for a loss of 19 of their own fighters during Big Week. Total Luftwaffe fighter losses during Big Week were about 355, but even more critical was the loss of about 150 pilots.

I Jagdkorps daytime Reich-defense operations in 1944

	January	February	March	April	May	June
Single-engine fighters available (average)	400	350	300	400	450	100
Twin-engine day fighters available	80	100	60	100	150	60
Night fighters available for daytime use	100	50	50	0	0	0
Sorties	2,306	2,861	2,226	4,522	3,618	1,310
Losses	122	299	240	395	384	179
Enemy aircraft claimed	179	310	302	514	530	179
Enemy aircraft encountered	7,158	10,452	16,612	20,337	27,700	11,900

Big Week represented a significant turning point in the air war over Germany. USAAF commanders had been concerned that some of the missions might result in the loss of up to 200 bombers; in fact the loss rate for each sortie (6 percent) had been lower than RAF Bomber Command casualties (6.6 percent) at the same time. The advent of long-range escort fighters had fundamentally changed the dynamics of the air battle. Big Week was a critical first step in gaining air superiority over Germany. Aircrew and aircraft losses were lower than in 1943, and by the late winter of 1944 there was a torrent of new aircraft and crews arriving from the United States, ensuring that the bomber and fighter force kept growing. The success of Big Week changed the framework for planning future operations. Instead of focusing on ways to evade German fighter strength, the focus now switched to directly challenging the Luftwaffe fighter force in the expectation of causing even further attrition.

The extent of the damage against the German aircraft plants was extensive, but not crippling. The Regensburg Messerschmitt plant was put out of action permanently; the Augsburg plant halted production for two weeks. The Leipzig plant had 160 new aircraft damaged, while at Gotha 74 aircraft were damaged or destroyed. Milch estimated that the attacks had cost the Luftwaffe the lost production of about 750 fighters. About 75 percent of the airframe and assembly plants had been damaged. However, the damage was primarily against the buildings, and only about 30 percent of the machine tools had been severely damaged. The attacks occurred at a point when the German industry was substantially ramping up single-engine fighter production. Although there was a short-term production decline in fighters in February 1944 because of the attacks and the destruction of many completed and partially completed aircraft on the ground, production rebounded in March. The hardest-hit plants had manufactured 1,555 aircraft in January, only 1,104 in February, but 1,638 in March. German officials later argued that the focus of the attacks was incorrect and that the aircraft-engine industry was a far more vulnerable one. In hindsight, this may be correct, but strategic bombing was still in its infancy and knowledge of the vulnerability of industries to bombing attack was far from complete.

Big Week created a crisis in the German aircraft industry, since it was appreciated that if the attacks continued then aircraft production could be derailed. There had already been some dispersion of plants prior to February, prompted in large measure by the 1943 USAAF attacks against plants in northwestern Germany such as Bremen. Following Big Week a major program of industrial dispersion was begun, with plans to disperse the 27 main airplane plants into 729 small plants. Likewise, the 59 aircraft-engine plants would be dispersed to 249 locations even though this industry had not yet been attacked on the scale of the assembly plants. The German aviation industry was successful in dispersing the industry to reduce its vulnerability to bombing attacks, but dispersion came at a cost. Plant dispersion made the industry more vulnerable to disruption in the transportation network since sub-components had to be shipped by rail or canal to other locations; Allied attacks on the transportation network later in the war created significant problems. Dispersion diluted the supervisory and technical talent in the industry and led to a rapid decline in aircraft quality in the later months of the war that severely impacted the actual combat utility of the aircraft. The loss of aircraft because of engine and other malfunctions increased alarmingly. Dispersion also required a larger workforce at a time when labor shortages were endemic, and forced the industry to make greater use of foreign forced labor. This led to sabotage problems, again depreciating aircraft quality.

The combined effects of bombing and the inefficiencies of dispersion did not derail the expansion in fighter production that Milch had started in the autumn of 1943. However, it did place a cap on the extent of fighter-production expansion. For example, Milch's "Defense of the Reich" Program 224 had anticipated building 3,327 single-engine fighters in July 1944; the actual total was 2,637. The February crisis prompted Milch to urge that Speer's armament industry take over control of fighter production in order to win the highest level of government priority. Speer used the February crisis to wrest control of aircraft production away from Göring, which largely settled the debate in favor of fighters and against further increases in bombers and flak. This led to the creation of the Fighter Staff (Jägerstab), led by Speer's ruthless right-hand man, Karl Saür. Fighter production was given first priority over any other sector of the war economy. Nevertheless, it was not until June that Hitler conceded that fighter production needed more resources and he finally authorized the substantial cutback of his favored bomber efforts. The politicization of the fighter-production effort had its drawbacks as well. Since so much emphasis was placed on the number of aircraft produced, other critical aspects of aircraft manufacture were short-changed. The sudden surge in fighter production in the spring of 1944 was partly accomplished by consuming large inventories of spare parts, and production that would have gone into manufacturing reserves of spares was diverted directly into production instead. In the long run this depreciated the value of assembled aircraft, as they could not be repaired because of a lack of parts. By the autumn of 1944 hundreds of Luftwaffe aircraft were stuck on the ground because of a widespread parts shortage.

The Big Week crisis provided the rationale for a variety of improvements in Luftflotte Reich that Schmid and other fighter commanders had been pushing for months. As mentioned earlier, the effort to improve ground-control-intercept finally took root with the switch to the enlarged and more powerful *Jagddivision* centers, which took over from the scattered *Jagdfliegerführer* and flak centers in the key areas of Germany. Sperrle continued to rebuff attempts at placing Luftflotte 3 under Reich control, but Schmid was able to enlarge I Jagdkorps' control by nibbling away at sectors away from the invasion front, such as Alsace, which came under central control. In the event, the forward-deployed fighter units in France and Belgium were becoming a less-valuable resource because of attrition, the transfer of squadrons back to Germany for Reich defense, and the priority given to Reich fighter squadrons for pilot and aircraft replacements. Several fighter units were drawn back into the Reich in early March 1944, not only to help in the Reich-defense efforts but also to locate them on bases less vulnerable to the increasingly active Allied tactical air forces. Sperrle's fighter force fell from about 450 to 150 aircraft. Schmid's I Jagdkorps headquarters moved from Zeist in the Netherlands back to Brunswick in Germany in mid-March 1944.

Big Week had demonstrated the effectiveness of massing fighters prior to attacking the bombers, and there were hopes that the improvements in GCI control would facilitate this. To deal with the escort fighters a new tactical practice was developed, with a Bf-109 Gruppe in each Geschwader being designated as a "*Höhengruppe*" (high group), while the more numerous Fw-190 Gruppen formed the main *Gefechtsverband* (combat formation). The Bf-109 was better suited to high-altitude fighter combat, so the *Höhengruppe* dealt with the escort fighters while the *Gefechtsverband* attacked the bombers. Another tactic to assist in the battle against the escort fighters was to make a greater effort to launch fighters over the Netherlands in order to attack escort fighters as early as possible in the hopes of forcing them to drop their tanks prematurely. Other technical improvements were delayed. The first Me-163 rocket-fighter unit had been deployed in January 1944, but this revolutionary aircraft suffered severe teething problems and required extensive training; the first few fighters were not declared operational until June 1944. The Me-262 program was delayed by the destruction of assembly jigs in the autumn 1943 bombing raids. But at the heart of its problems was its revolutionary jet engine, which was on the "bleeding edge" of technology and not yet suitable for mass production or operational deployment until after the summer of 1944.

CONFRONTATION: BERLIN, MARCH 1944

Buoyed by Big Week's success, Doolittle selected Berlin as the next major target for the Eighth Air Force. While there were numerous aircraft-industry targets in the area, the main intent of the raid was to stir up the Luftwaffe in the hopes of accelerating the war of attrition. The Eighth Air Force was frustrated in its attempts to attack Berlin in the first week of March. An attack on March 4 encountered such poor weather that most of the attack force bombed secondary targets in the Ruhr, though some P-38 escort fighters reached Berlin. The first major attack was staged on March 6. Aside from some diversionary feints by Ninth Air Force medium bombers to draw away

Lufflotte 3 fighters, the bombers' path was making directly for Berlin. A total of 814 bombers took off, of which 702 reached the target areas around Berlin. Their fighter escort was 801 Eighth Air Force fighters, plus additional support from the RAF and Ninth Air Force. All three divisions of I Jagdkorps were committed, with some 328 fighters participating, and Schmid also was allotted support from the 7. Jagddivision; total Luftwaffe action involved 528 sorties with 369 actually engaging in combat.

The air battles rivaled the intensity of the Schweinfurt missions a half-year earlier. The first confrontation took place when a large *Gefechtsverband* of fighters from both 2. and 3. Jagddivisionen hit the 3rd Bombardment Division over Haseluenne. During the fighting, some 20 B-17 bombers were shot down at a cost of about 12 German fighters. In the meantime another *Gefechtsverband* from 1. Jagddivision formed up closer to Magdeburg, including a large concentration of 40 Bf-110 and Me-410 heavy fighters. Although their rocket attacks against the 1st Bombardment Division caused little damage, they disrupted the combat boxes prior to cannon attacks in the vicinity of Tangerhuette. In this case, the P-51 escorts from the 357th Group intervened more effectively than at Haseluenne, and 16 of the 41 heavy fighters were lost; in total, the Luftwaffe lost 23 fighters in this mêlée while downing 11 B-17s and 4 P-51s. The Berlin corridor was heavily saturated with flak, which discouraged fighter actions, though a number of German night fighters and scattered day fighters continued their attacks. Flak claimed 13 bombers and one fighter that day, and contributed to several other losses. By the end of the mission that afternoon it had become the Eighth Air Force's bloodiest air battle on record, with some 69 B-17s and 11 escort fighters lost. Luftwaffe losses were 66 aircraft shot down or damaged beyond repair, or one out of every five that had engaged in combat. The losses were especially heavy in the twin-engine units with the Bf-110 and Me-410 day fighters losing 40 percent of those participating and the Bf-110 night fighters losing 9 out 18. The vast majority of Luftwaffe losses were because of the escort fighters. Both sides claimed the Berlin battle as a victory with the German press trumpeting the loss of 140 American bombers. Actual bomb damage on the ground had been light as cloud cover and combat interfered with targeting. Yet in spite of the heavy losses, the Eighth Air Force had scored a major propaganda victory, conducting an assault on the German capital in broad daylight. The loss rate at around 10 percent was heavier than average, but not enough to discourage further attacks.

The Eighth Air Force campaign against Berlin was relentless. Two days later, on March 8, 623 bombers attacked the Erkner ball-bearing plant in Berlin's southern suburbs. The attack followed the same path as before over northern Germany, and I Jagdkorps responded in the same fashion, first forming up a large *Gefechtsverband* near Brunswick from Jagdgeschwader 1 and Jagdgeschwader 11. The scale of the German attack was smaller than before because of the number of damaged aircraft, and only 282 fighters were launched. US losses were 40 bombers and 34 fighters; German losses were 42 fighters. On March 9 the bombers returned to Berlin and the Hanover area with 490 bomber sorties. This time I Jagdkorps did not even attempt to respond, hampered by casualties and the thick cloud cover; US losses were 11 bombers to flak and weather. Much the same was the case on March 11 when a smaller attack by 124 B-17 bombers hit Münster with no fighter opposition.

The next large operation was a deep attack against Augsburg in southern Germany on March 16 with 675 bombers and 868 escort fighters. This time both I Jagdkorps and the autonomous 7. Jagddivision responded with 266 fighter sorties. It was a very bad day for the Luftwaffe twin-engine fighters and Zerstörergeschwader 76 was jumped by Mustangs whilst forming up, losing 23 of its 77 fighters. Losses at the end of the day were 23 US bombers and 10 escorts; German losses were 46 fighters, and Zerstörergeschwader 76 was pulled out of combat.

The Fifteenth Air Force had been restricted in its participation in Operation *Argument* because of its frequent commitment in support of the Anzio beachhead, as well as weather-related issues. An important indirect contribution to the struggle was a campaign against German and Italian fighter bases in the Po Valley in northern Italy, which had been intercepting flights into southern Germany. The Fifteenth Air Force's first attack into the Reich since February was on March 17 against Vienna; the response from Jagdfliegerführer Ostmark was weak, and consisted of a handful of Hungarian Bf-109 and Me-210 fighters.

A combined attack was launched on March 18, with Eighth Air Force striking a broad range of targets in south-central Germany including Oberpfaffenhofen, Munich, and Friedrichshafen; Fifteenth Air Force directed its attention to Luftwaffe bases around Udine in northern Italy. Luftwaffe

A B-17G of the 352nd Bombardment Group moments before releasing its bombs over Berlin on the March 9, 1944, mission. (NARA)

LEFT
The "Bloody 100th" developed a reputation as the 3rd Bombardment Division's unluckiest unit. During the March 6 mission to Berlin it lost 15 bombers, with one squadron entirely wiped out. This remarkable photo taken in September 1944 shows a B-17G of the 100th Bombardment Group with an Me-410 heavy fighter closing in on its tail. (NARA)

RIGHT
"Flak so thick you could walk on it." A B-17G of 534th Squadron, 381st Bombardment Group, flies through a heavy flak barrage on the way to its target. This aircraft was lost on March 24, 1944, after receiving a direct flak hit in the rear fuselage that nearly severed the tail. The pilot managed to get the aircraft back over the English Channel before the crew bailed out. (NARA)

resistance was moderate with 47 bombers lost from all causes and US fighters claiming 36 German fighters. The Fifteenth Air Force returned to Austria the next day and faced fighter opposition in northern Italy as well as from Jagdfliegerführer Ostmark, losing 21 bombers. The Italy based force still did not have the same degree of escort coverage as did Eighth Air Force, though steps were under way to reinforce it. The Eighth Air Force returned to Berlin on March 22 in overcast weather and conducted radar bombing through the cloud; I Jagdkorps made no effort at all to intercept under these weather conditions and with the battered state of its force. An attack the following day against aircraft plants in the Brunswick and Münster areas brought a much more intense response from I Jagdkorps, which launched 259 aircraft from all three divisions. A strong tailwind had pushed the bombers ahead of schedule for the escort fighters, allowing the German fighters about 15 minutes of uninterrupted attacks on the bombers. When the P-51s finally appeared, the situation quickly reversed and among the casualties that day was the commander of Jagdgeschwader 3, Oberst Wolf Wilcke, a renowned ace with 192 victories. It was one of the first missions where the twin-engine fighters did not participate. Zerstörergeschwader 76 had been withdrawn because of heavy casualties, and Zerstörergeschwader 26 was moved to Prussia and out of harm's way. There were plans to revive the units with the new Me-410 fighter. American casualties were 29 bombers and 5 fighters; I Jagdkorps casualties were 26 fighters shot down or damaged beyond repair. The Brunswick mission was the last major attack in March, although the Eighth Air Force conducted numerous missions over France and the Netherlands when the weather over Germany was too poor for operations.

I Jagdkorps' commander, "Beppo" Schmid, later assessed the lessons of the March fighting. "American losses during Big Week had no effect whatsoever on American operations. American air forces captured air supremacy over the entire Reich except for the more distant east. The bombing of Berlin and Munich meant the collapse of German air power."

BEYOND OPERATION *POINTBLANK*

The Combined Bomber Offensive and Operation *Pointblank* formally ended on April 1, 1944. This marked a command transition of the strategic bomber forces from control by the Combined Chiefs of Staff to control by Eisenhower's SHAEF (Supreme Headquarters Allied Expeditionary Force).

Under the original scheme, USSTAF switched from Portal's command to a new AEAF (Allied Expeditionary Air Force) command under Air Marshall Trafford Leigh-Mallory. Arnold and Spaatz were not happy about the switch, both because of concerns about Leigh-Mallory's judgment as well as serious disagreements over tactics and strategy. Leigh-Mallory's leadership was further undermined by his strong disagreements with his fellow RAF commander, Arthur Harris of Bomber Command. While Spaatz understood that at some point the USSTAF would be taken off its strategic missions to support Operation *Overlord*, Harris was adamant that Bomber Command be reserved for strategic missions and that support for *Overlord* should be undertaken solely by the tactical air forces, which were better suited to the task. To mediate the disputes Eisenhower turned to Arthur Tedder, his RAF air deputy who had served with him in the Mediterranean theater in 1943 and who served as Deputy Supreme Commander AEF for Operation *Overlord*.

Spaatz tried to convince Eisenhower and Tedder that the USSTAF had enough strength in the spring of 1944 to simultaneously engage in a continued strategic campaign into Germany while also conducting the necessary missions to support *Overlord*. The Ninth Air Force had been specifically deployed in Britain to conduct tactical missions, which gave the Eighth Air Force freedom to continue its strategic missions. At the heart of the AEAF's mission for the USAAF and RAF strategic bombers was the "Transportation Plan." It had been conceived by Professor Solly Zuckerman, and it aimed to sever the main rail links between Germany and the Normandy battlefield by concentrated attacks on rail choke points such as bridges and marshalling yards. Spaatz did not feel that the Transportation Plan represented the best use of the Eighth Air Force, and offered his own alternative, dubbed the "Oil Plan."

The highest-scoring USAAF fighter pilot during Operation *Pointblank* was Captain Don Gentile of the 336th Fighter Squadron, 4th Fighter Group, seen here with his P-51B "Shangri-La." Gentile had joined the RAF in 1941 and served in the Eagle Squadron; in April 1944 he was credited with 27.8 kills in USAAF service plus two in RAF service. (NARA)

The Oil Plan was intended to be a continuation of Operation *Pointblank*, but with updated priorities. Since most of the aircraft-assembly plants had been bombed during *Pointblank*, the emphasis would shift to the German fuel industry, and especially to the synthetic-fuel plants that provided all of the Luftwaffe's high-octane aviation fuel. Destruction of 14 synthetic-fuel plants and 13 refineries would eliminate 80 percent of production, 60 percent of refining capability, and substantially reduce available German fuel supplies. Spaatz's resistance to the Transportation Plan was echoed from other influential corners, notably Field Marshal Alan Brooke, chief of the British Imperial General Staff. To complicate the debate further, in mid-April Churchill began to push for an acceleration of the campaign against the suspected German V-weapon "Crossbow" launch sites. These had already been targeted by the Eighth Air Force under its "Noball" program when weather over Germany prevented missions there. However, Churchill was pushing this mission as the top priority over Luftwaffe, oil, or transportation targets, to the consternation of Spaatz and Harris who believed the attacks to be a complete waste of heavy bombers. Indeed, the devastating attacks on the original V-1 "ski" sites had forced the Luftwaffe to shift to other basing options, but construction continued at the ski sites to distract Allied bombers and cause them to continue to waste bombs attacking them.

In the end, the targeting decisions eventually became a mixture of all of these various objectives. Weather played a critical factor in any precision-bombing mission, and as often as not a bad-weather day over Germany left alternate targeting opportunities in France. During the third week of April, after heated debate, Eisenhower gave Spaatz permission to begin his oil campaign. When pressed about hitting the high-priority Crossbow targets at a meeting on April 20, Tedder and Spaatz agreed to a compromise under

Death of a B-17. This gun-camera footage from a Bf-110G-2 from June 1944 shows the approach from the rear from a range of about 600m. The first frame shows a 30mm strike on the inboard right engine while the following frame to the right shows a hit on the tail. As the Bf-110 closed on its victim, it can be seen that the cannon had knocked out the rear- and belly-gun positions and set the left inboard engine on fire. (Author's collection)

The threat of strafing USAAF escort fighters forced the Luftwaffe to disperse and camouflage their fighter bases, as is seen with this Bf-109 under repair along a tree line near the Stendal airbase. (NARA)

which the Eighth Air Force would hit Crossbow targets on the first day of clear weather, and then would be free to spend two missions hitting oil targets in Germany.

While the targeting debate was in full swing, the USTAAF's April missions were a mixture of Luftwaffe aircraft plants in Germany and Noball/Crossbow targets in France. After Tedder's prodding, the V-1 sites in Pas-de-Calais began to receive large-scale strikes starting on April 20, 1944. Prior to this mission, most of the Eighth Air Force Crossbow attacks had been against a handful of Crossbow "heavy" sites at Watten, Wizernes, and Siracourt, which were small, discrete targets that could be attacked by only relatively small formations. Eighth Air Force missions in April totaled over 10,000 bomber sorties, delivering over 23,000 tons of bombs. German industrial targets were the primary objectives, accounting for about 71 percent of tonnage, while Crossbow targets accounted for about 27 percent.

HITTING THE ACHILLES HEEL: THE OIL CAMPAIGN, MAY 1944

After the April 20 agreement with Tedder, the Eighth Air Force had to wait until May 12 for sufficiently clear weather. The attack included 886 bombers from all three divisions and 735 Eighth and 245 Ninth Air Force fighters, targeting 13 separate fuel facilities. By early May Schmidt had convinced Stumpff to concentrate all the fighter-direction centers, including the previously autonomous 7. Jagddivision under I Jagdkorps. Although the day-fighter squadrons had not been substantially enlarged after the costly February–March fighting, the "*Wilde Sau*" (Wild Boar) single-engine night-fighter squadrons were thrown into the day battle. As a result, the Luftwaffe response on May 12 was the first time that a concentrated effort by the entire Reich force was achieved, with 419 fighters participating in the first wave and 51 in the second wave. This was especially important as the USAAF targets were scattered over a wide area and required exceptional co-ordination on the part of air defense. A massive *Gefechstverband* was created in the Frankfurt-am-Main area, which included Jagdgeschwader 3 of the 1.

Jagddivision, Jagdgeschwader 11 of the 2. Jagddivision, and Jagdgeschwader 27 of the 7. Jagddivision. The 3. Jagddivision and "*Wilde Sau*" fighters were hit by US escort fighters while climbing to formation altitude and so were not especially effective against the bomber stream near Giessen and Mannheim. The Luftwaffe fighters and flak cost the attacking force 46 bombers and 7 escorts, but Luftwaffe losses were severe, including 65 fighters. Leadership losses were also grave. Oberst Walter Oesau, commander of Jagdgeschwader 1 and one of the Luftwaffe's top aces, had been killed the day before, and on May 12 both Major Gunther Rall of I/Jagdgeschwader 11 and Hauptmann Rolf Hermichen of II/Jagdgeschwader 11 were wounded.

The May 12 attacks on the hydrogenation plants had been effective: the Zeitz plant was hardest hit and lost 16 weeks of output; the Brüx and Tröglitz plants were shut down and lost seven weeks' output while the Böhlen and Leuna plants lost half or more of their capacity. Speer reported to Hitler on May 19 that: "The enemy has struck us at one of our weakest points. If they persist at it this time, then we will soon no longer have any fuel production worth mentioning. Our one hope is that the other side has an air force general staff as scatterbrained as ours." Schmid was equally grim in his assessment, judging that "On this day, the technological war was decided."

An attempt to attack the hydrogenation plants in Silesia in eastern Germany on May 13 was largely frustrated, but a massive May 28 attack of 1,341 bombers and 1,224 fighters against a large number of fuel-related targets and aircraft led to another major air battle. I Jagdkorps put up 333 fighters, which were vectored into a great *Gefechstverband* over Magdeburg. Even Jagdfliegerführer Ostmark from Austria was called into the fight. Oberstleutnant Rüdiger von Kirchmayr formed up a group from the 3. Jagddivision and two more formations from the 1. and 7. Jagddivisionen joined it, forming an angry swarm of 180 Fw-190 and Bf-109 fighters, while three Bf-109 *Gruppen* formed into a high-altitude group to deal with the escorts. The German formation hit the 390th Bombardment Group, but was then in turn hit by P-51 Mustangs of the 357th Fighter Group, which claimed 33 German fighters in its attack. Several more escort groups joined the mêlée. The day's attack was again costly on both sides, with 33 bombers and 12 fighters lost to Luftwaffe fighters and flak; German losses were between 52 and 78 shot down or damaged beyond repair. The effect of the bombing on the oil plants was not as dramatic as on May 12, with only the Zeitz plant being severely damaged. Nevertheless, the May 28 battle showed the diminishing ability of the Luftwaffe to deal with bomber attacks.

The Eighth Air Force returned the next day with a deep attack against the Pölitz plant near Stettin on the Baltic coast, as well as a variety of other targets deep in Prussia and western Poland. The bomber stream totaled 993 bombers and 1,265 escort fighters. Because of the depth of the attack, the 2nd Bombardment Division split off to hit Pölitz while the other divisions hit aviation plants in central Germany. At the same time, the Fifteenth Air Force struck targets in southern Germany and Austria. I Jagdkorps put up 275 fighters and Jagdfliegerführer Ostpreussen (East Prussia) and Jagdfliegerführer Schlesien (Silesia) added a further 76 against the Eighth Air Force bomber streams; 208 of these saw combat. The 7. Jagddivision and Jagdfliegerführer Ostmark headed for the Fifteenth Air Force with 101 more fighters. The northern air battles led to the loss of 37 bombers, mainly the B-24s near the Baltic, as well as ten fighters; German fighter losses were 57 shot down or damaged beyond repair. In the southern battles the 7. Jagddivision claimed seven bombers for a loss of 24 fighters shot down or damaged beyond repair. The Pölitz plant was put out of operation for two months.

Besides overhead reconnaissance photographs of the extensive damage from the May oil-bombing attacks, Allied intelligence quickly began to pick up strong evidence from signals intercepts that the oil campaign was having a significant impact. On May 14 Luftflotte 3 in France was informed by radio that nine flak batteries were being diverted from the Russian front to protect the hydrogenation plants at Pölitz and Blechhammer. On May 19 Berlin informed the Kreigsmarine headquarters in Paris that there would be considerable reductions in fuel in June because of the attacks, and Black Sea command was warned that they would receive no fuel at all in June. These reports were so encouraging that Eighth Air Force badgered RAF Bomber

The Fifteenth Air Force was assigned oil targets in southern Germany, Austria, Romania, and Hungary. "Fertile Myrtle," a B-24G-16 of the 726th Squadron, 451st Bombardment Group, is seen here during a mission against oil refineries near Budapest with a pall of smoke rising from the target. This aircraft was lost over Austria on September 23, 1944. (NARA)

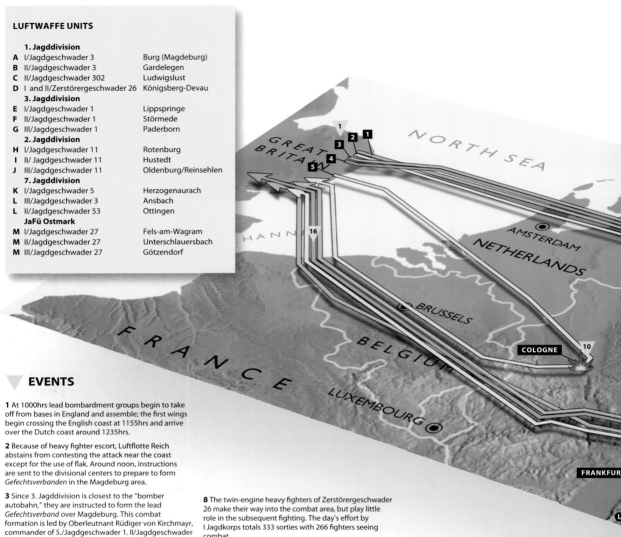

LUFTWAFFE UNITS

1. Jagddivision
A I/Jagdgeschwader 3 Burg (Magdeburg)
B II/Jagdgeschwader 3 Gardelegen
C II/Jagdgeschwader 302 Ludwigslust
D I and II/Zerstörergeschwader 26 Königsberg-Devau
3. Jagddivision
E I/Jagdgeschwader 1 Lippspringe
F II/Jagdgeschwader 1 Störmede
G III/Jagdgeschwader 1 Paderborn
2. Jagddivision
H I/Jagdgeschwader 11 Rotenburg
I II/ Jagdgeschwader 11 Hustedt
J III/Jagdgeschwader 11 Oldenburg/Reinsehlen
7. Jagddivision
K I/Jagdgeschwader 5 Herzogenaurach
L III/Jagdgeschwader 3 Ansbach
L II/Jagdgeschwader 53 Ottingen
JaFü Ostmark
M I/Jagdgeschwader 27 Fels-am-Wagram
M II/Jagdgeschwader 27 Unterschlauersbach
M III/Jagdgeschwader 27 Götzendorf

▼ EVENTS

1 At 1000hrs lead bombardment groups begin to take off from bases in England and assemble; the first wings begin crossing the English coast at 1155hrs and arrive over the Dutch coast around 1235hrs.

2 Because of heavy fighter escort, Luftflotte Reich abstains from contesting the attack near the coast except for the use of flak. Around noon, instructions are sent to the divisional centers to prepare to form *Gefechtsverbanden* in the Magdeburg area.

3 Since 3. Jagddivision is closest to the "bomber autobahn," they are instructed to form the lead *Gefechtsverband* over Magdeburg. This combat formation is led by Oberleutnant Rüdiger von Kirchmayr, commander of 5./Jagdgeschwader 1. II/Jagdgeschwader 1 is assigned as the *Höhengruppe*, tasked with intercepting escort fighters.

4 The 2. Jagddivision, based principally around Jagdgeschwader 11, beings to form up its units behind the 3. Jagddivision lead, with II/Jagdgeschwader 11 forming the *Höhengruppe* to deal with the escorts.

5 The 1. Jagddivision, consisting of Jagdgeschwader 3 and the single-seat night fighters of Jagdgeschwader 302, begin to join up with the other two divisions over Magdeburg, with I/Jagdgeschwader 3 assigned as top cover.

6 The 7. Jagddivision out of southern Germany arrives before noon and contributes three *Gruppen* to the expanding *Gefechtsverband*.

7 I Jagdkorps' headquarters instructs the *Gefechtsverband* to avoid the lead bomber formations, which are apt to be the best protected, and to attack the trailing units. The attacks begin in force around 1300hrs, with the 390th Bombardment Group, 13th Combat Wing of Force 2 bearing the brunt of the initial assault. At this stage, I Jagdkorps has managed to mass about 180 Bf-109 and Fw-190 fighters.

8 The twin-engine heavy fighters of Zerstörergeschwader 26 make their way into the combat area, but play little role in the subsequent fighting. The day's effort by I Jagdkorps totals 333 sorties with 266 fighters seeing combat.

9 Jagdfliegerführer Ostmark adds three *Gruppen* of fighters out of Austria, which are directed against the 94th Combat Wing of Force 2 heading for Dessau.

10 Force 5 stages a diversionary attack on Cologne around 1310hrs, but attracts few German defenders. This attack includes the use of the secret GB-1 guided glide bomb by the 41st Combat Wing.

11 Force 2 begins its bombing runs around 1400hrs, with the 4th and 45th Combat Wings hitting an ordnance depot in Königsborn and the 13th Combat Wing hitting the Braunkohle-Benzin AG synthetic-fuel plant in Magdeburg.

12 Force 1 begins its dispersed attacks on Junkers AG aircraft plants in Dessau by the 1st Combat Wing around 1415hrs, while the 40th Combat Wing attacks the Braunkohle-Benzin AG synthetic-fuel plant in Ruhland.

13 Force 3 hits the IG Farbin AG synthetic-fuel plant at Merseburg/Leuna with the 2nd Combat Wing at around 1430hrs, while the neighboring 92nd and 93rd Combat Wings from Force 4 hit the Wintershall AG synthetic-fuel plant at Lutzkendorf.

14 The 14th and 96th Combat Wings of Force 3 bomb the Braunkohle-Benzin AG synthetic-fuel plant at Zeitz at around 1500hrs, the last of the primary targets. Total flak activity for the day totals 399 heavy batteries firing 32,000 rounds and 63 light batteries firing 16,770 rounds.

15 The four task forces exit the main target area, but some units attack targets of opportunity on the way home, for example the 1st Combat Wing at Frankfurt around 1545hrs.

16 The attack force begins to leave the coast at around 1700hrs. I Jagdkorps claims 36 bombers and 11 fighters plus 20 from flak. Actual USAAF casualties for the day are 32 bombers and 14 fighters. I Jagdkorps losses are 78 aircraft shot down (44) or damaged beyond repair (34) and 17 destroyed on the ground.

ATTACK ON LUFTWAFFE FUEL PRODUCTION: MAY 28, 1944
The Luftwaffe concentrates its fighters but fails in the face of heavy USAAF fighter escort

USAAF UNITS

	Task Force	Bombardment division	Bombardment groups	Fighter groups, penetration support	Fighter groups, target support	Fighter groups, withdrawal support
1	Force 1	1st Bombardment Division	91st, 92nd, 303rd, 306th, 379th, 381st, 401st, and 457th Bombardment Groups	78th Fighter Group	4th, 352nd, 355th, and 363th Fighter Group	50th, 358th, and 367th Fighter Group
2	Force 2	3rd Bombardment Division	94th, 95th, 96th, 100th, 385th, 388th, 390th, 447th, and 452nd Bombardment Groups	356th Fighter Group	354th, 357th, and 359th Fighter Groups	36th, 362nd, and 474th Fighter Group
3	Force 3	2nd Bombardment Division	44th, 93rd, 389th, 392nd, 445th, 446th, 448th, 453rd, 458th, 466th, 467th, 492nd, and 492nd Bombardment Groups	353rd Fighter Group	20th and 361st Fighter Groups	370th and 373rd Fighter Group
4	Force 4	3rd Bombardment Division	34th, 487th, and 486th Bombardment Groups	479th Fighter Group	55th and 339th Fighter Groups	19th, 65th, 129th, and 306th Fighter Groups; 315th Squadron (RAF)
5	Force 5	1st Bombardment Division	303rd, 379th, and 384th Bombardment Groups	364th Fighter Group	406th Fighter Group	406th Fighter Group

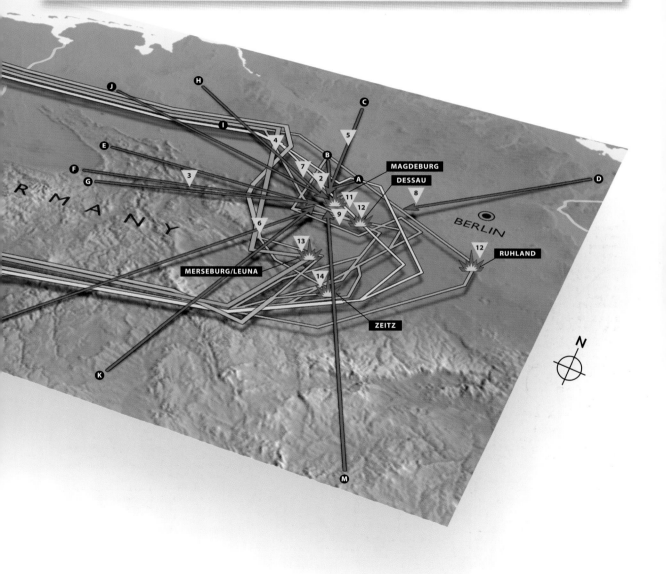

MAGDEBURG

DESSAU

BERLIN

RUHLAND

MERSEBURG/LEUNA

ZEITZ

GERMANY

Command to join the attacks, and a mission on the night of June 12–13 against Gelsenkirchen-Nordstern Bergius was the most destructive of the war, accounting for the destruction of 200,000 tons of synthetic fuel and depriving the German war effort of a further 1,000 tons of aviation fuel every day for an indefinite period of time before the facility could be repaired. In fact, subsequent attacks kept it inoperative. Decrypts on June 7, one day after the Normandy landings, disclosed that Berlin had warned units in France that fuel would be restricted to only the most vital Luftwaffe units, that the Wehrmacht strategic reserve was finally being tapped, and that the situation was so catastrophic that July allotments could not be planned and that units should plan on depending on available stocks and whatever stocks could be scraped together in the meantime. This Ultra decrypt was judged by the Chiefs of Staff to be "one of the most important pieces of information we have yet received," and they urged Churchill not to wait but to reassign the combined strategic bomber force against the German oil industry as quickly as possible to precipitate its collapse. Allied intelligence estimated that German synthetic-fuel capacity had been reduced from 1,200,000 tons per month to 670,000 tons, and that the Wehrmacht required at least 1,000,000 tons per month for operational efficiency. Allied intelligence had recognized that it had finally found a vital target that was exceptionally vulnerable to bomber attack

Luftwaffe day-fighter/flak claims, January–June 1944*

Month	Days with large incursions	Fighter sorties	Heavy-fighter sorties	Certain fighter claims	Certain flak claims	Probable fighter claims	Probable flak claims
January	9	2,467	1,294	288	28	89	13
February	12	3,591	808	529	120	154	17
March	18	3,347	400	355	119	71	37
April	18	4,470	541	554	163	122	40
May	19	4,558	291	550	224	67	36
June	11	1,082	562	156	92	32	21
Total	87	19,515	3,896	2,432	746	535	164

*Including both Luftflotte 3 and Luftflotte Reich units

Luftwaffe casualties, day fighters in the West, January–June 1944

Month	Dead	Missing	Wounded	Aircraft destroyed	Missing	Damaged
January	133	27	104	209	24	107
February	171	54	141	309	46	155
March	115	104	103	269	87	163
April	209	61	125	302	51	151
May	210	66	186	419	68	243
June	114	27	58	144	22	75
Total	952	339	717	1,652	298	894

Doolittle's decision to free up the escort fighters also initiated frequent attacks on Luftwaffe fighter bases. This is a camouflaged revetment at the Detmold airfield littered with the wreckage of Bf-109G fighters. (NARA)

THE PAYOFF: OPERATION *OVERLORD* AND BEYOND

From the USAAF's perspective, Operation *Pointblank* had been a costly success. Although its goal was reached, it had not occurred in the way the USAAF had expected. The initial conception had been that "self-defending" bombers could devastate the German aircraft plants, ending fighter production and thereby winning air superiority. In fact, both of these tenets proved to be false. The "self-defending" bomber proved to be a failure in the face of tough Luftwaffe opposition. The senior leadership of the USAAF proved pragmatic and adaptable under the circumstances, abandoned their cherished doctrine, and vigorously supported a crash program to field a substantial deep-escort force by early 1944. The combination of fuel-extension programs for the P-47 and P-38 and the arrival of the superior P-51 were important ingredients in the eventual success of the escort fighter. However, they were not the only factor. Arnold, Doolittle, and Kepner also switched the tactical doctrine from close-bomber support to mixed tactics encompassing free-ranging attacks on German fighter formations and airbases. The results were dramatic and proved to be a tipping point in the air campaign over Germany.

The USAAF expected that precision-bombing attacks against German fighter-assembly plants could shrink or collapse the Luftwaffe fighter force. This proved to be a chimera. German fighter production actually increased from 1943 to 1944. This aspect of the USAAF plan was unsuccessful in part because Allied intelligence had little reliable intelligence on the German aircraft industry and was not aware of Milch's fighter-production expansion plan. Although Operation *Pointblank* failed to cut Luftwaffe fighter production, it did manage to place a limit on the expansion planned by Milch. For example, Milch's Program 224 from October 1, 1943, anticipated the production of 13,400 single-engine fighters in the first half of 1944 when actually only 6,650 to 9,485 were produced. The scale of German fighter production in 1944 is more obscure than generally recognized. The post-war US Strategic Bombing Survey on the aviation industry indicated that German fighter production more than doubled from 1943 to 1944, going from 11,738 to 28,529 according to Speer's ministry's data. What has not been as widely noted was that a separate report by the Military Analysis Division found that German statistics on fighter production were exaggerated for internal political reasons and probably overstated German fighter production by as much as 30 percent. Accounting tricks made the fighter program seem like a miracle to Hitler, but the purported increase in new fighters manufactured did not translate into comparable growth in operational-fighter strength.

Regardless of the effectiveness of the attack on the plants, by December 1943 General Arnold and the USAAF leadership had shifted from a purely industrial approach to a broader focus on attrition that encompassed attacks on the plants, attrition through fighter battles, and through attacks on Luftwaffe airbases. The results on the Luftwaffe were dramatic. Luftwaffe leadership was unprepared for escort fighters that could range so deeply into Germany. The heavy-fighter force, even with the new Me-410, was annihilated. The single-engine fighter force, in spite of better tactics and equipment, was unable to deal with the new escort fighters because of the severe decline in pilot quality. In May 1944 the average I Jagdkorps operational strength was 450 single-engine and 150 heavy fighters; combat losses were 419 aircraft, or about 70 percent of the force. The attrition rate per mission was a staggering 11 percent; although the lost fighters could be replaced, the pilots could not. This situation only grew worse, and the overall

Spaatz argued with Eisenhower that the medium bombers of the Ninth Air Force were better suited to the "Transportation Plan" than the heavy bombers of the Eighth Air Force. Here, a pair of A-20G Havoc bombers of the 671st Squadron, 416th Bombardment Group, hit the Domfront rail station on the Orne River during the June 1944 attacks. (NARA)

average monthly loss rate for fighters in the West went from 45 percent monthly in 1943 to a gruesome 82 percent in 1944. The Luftwaffe single-engine fighter force suffered catastrophic losses from the last quarter of 1943, with 1,052 fighters lost, 2,180 in the first quarter of 1944, 3,057 in the second quarter of 1944, and a staggering 4,043 fighters in the third quarter of 1944. To put this in some perspective, the Luftwaffe lost more single-engine fighters in the West from July to September 1944 than they lost in two whole years on the Russian front from September 1942 to September 1944.

Luftwaffe fighter-pilot losses were grim. For example, 462 crewmen were lost in May, including 275 dead and 185 wounded, or about three out of every five. When Feldmarschall Hugo von Sperrle canvassed his command in July 1944, he found that with rare exceptions only group and squadron commanders had operational experience of over 6 months. Of the remainder, a small percentage had been in combat for three months but the majority had been in combat for only 8–30 days.

The steady destruction of the Luftwaffe fighter force made the 8th Air Force increasingly brazen in its camouflage practices, completely foregoing camouflage paint on many aircraft later in 1944, such as these B-17Gs of the 532nd Squadron, 381st Bombardment Group. (NARA)

Luftwaffe single-engine fighter losses by front: December 1942 to September 1944

	Dec 27, 1942	March 31, 1943	June 30, 1943	Sept 30, 1943	Dec 31, 1943	March 31, 1944	June 30, 1944	Sept 30, 1944	Total
Reich Defense/West	324	629	1,048	1,412	1,052	2,180	3,057	4,043	**13,745**
Mediterranean front	175	338	564	751	567	520	512	188	**3,615**
Russian front	298	343	565	631	335	391	511	705	**3,779**
Total	797	1,310	2,177	2,794	1,954	3,091	4,080	4,936	**21,139**
Reich/West percentage	40.6	48.0	48.1	50.5	53.8	70.5	74.9	81.9	**65.0**

The effects of the air battles over Germany in January–May 1944 were evident in the skies over Normandy on D-Day, June 6, 1944. Luftflotte 3 in France had been held back from some of the worst May 1944 air battles in hopes of conserving its strength for the expected invasion. Nevertheless, its paltry forces could do nothing in the face of the massive scope of Allied missions on D-Day, which totaled about 13,700 sorties. The Allies had total air superiority and the Luftwaffe fighter force was almost completely ineffective against this vast armada. The fighter units of Luftflotte 3 on D-Day claimed to have shot down 24 Allied aircraft out of the approximately 130 lost that day

to all causes; Luftwaffe fighter losses were 16. The emaciated state of the Luftwaffe fighter force in the West was largely attributable to the Operation *Pointblank* air battles of the previous several months. It took Luftflotte 3 the remaining three weeks of June to match the number of sorties that the Allies had conducted on D-Day alone, a 20-fold difference in sortie rates.

Luftwaffe strength in France increased in June and July as more units were pushed forward from the Reich defense force. However, the Luftwaffe never managed to seriously challenge Allied air supremacy in the summer and autumn battles either over France or Germany. While the Luftwaffe sometimes staged major surge operations, for example the attacks on the Seine River crossings in mid-August 1944, they were never able to seriously contest Allied air dominance. In mid-August Hitler was so frustrated at the ineffectiveness of the Luftwaffe Reich-defense force that he instructed Galland to deploy the Luftflotte Reich units to the west in a tactical role, and told Speer to cut fighter production in favor of flak. The German war industries were in an irreversible descent to annihilation.

Regardless of the success in suppressing Luftwaffe fighters, German flak remained a dangerous threat. This B-24, named "Little Warrior," of the 862nd Bomber Squadron, 493rd Bombardment Group, piloted by Lieutenant Jon Hansen, was hit in its #3 engine by flak on a mission against the aircraft-engine plant near Fallersleben on June 29, 1944. The flak damage ignited the fuel tanks and most of the crew was killed in the ensuing crash. A memorial to the crew of the "Little Warrior" stands today outside the elementary school in McKee's Rock, Pennsylvania. (NARA)

THE BATTLEFIELD TODAY

Unlike land campaigns, the battlefields of an air campaign are significantly more ephemeral and diverse. Innumerable locations on the ground can be linked to Operation *Pointblank*, including the airbases of both sides, the flak and radar sites, command posts and headquarters, the target areas in Germany, and military cemeteries and memorials in both Britain and Germany. There has been far less interest in memorializing the war in Germany than in Britain, and military museums commemorating World War II have been politically unacceptable. There are ample commemorations of the air campaign in Britain, notably the American Air Museum, part of the Imperial War Museum in Duxford, England, which is dedicated to the long connection between the US Air Force and Britain. There are numerous other museums and memorials in the UK with connections to the wartime Eighth Air Force, as well as many museums and memorials with Eighth Air Force connections in the United States.

Aside from the buildings, bases, and memorials associated with the campaign, surviving aircraft are probably the most popular form of remembrance. I have always felt the closest connection to the air campaigns

After sitting outside in the Memphis area for many years, the "Memphis Belle" began restoration at the National Museum of the US Air Force in 2005. It is seen here in 2009 while undergoing sheet-metal work. (USAF)

while visiting air museums holding surviving veteran aircraft. For me, sitting in the cockpit of a Bf-109, crawling into the cramped gun turret of a B-17, or peering into the bomb-bay of a B-24 provides a closer link to the past than visiting airbases or other sites. A handful of the *Pointblank* aircraft still survive. The B-17 "Memphis Belle" sat outdoors in the Memphis area for a half-century and is now under restoration at the US Air Force Museum at Wright-Patterson Air Force Base. Few if any German aircraft from the *Pointblank* campaign still survive, though there are representative Bf-109s, FW-190s, and other types in many collections. Wreckage of crashed German fighters and American bombers continues to be pulled from the Dutch polders below the "bomber autobahn" over the Netherlands during land-reclamation projects.

Few actual participants of the 1944 air campaigns have survived, so their legacy has been memorialized by marking surviving aircraft with their insignia. This former Indian Air Force B-24J is preserved in exquisite condition at the Pima Air & Space Museum in Tucson, Arizona, in the markings of a B-24H-25-FO of the 704th Bomb Squadron, 446th Bombardment Group. (Author's collection)

FURTHER READING

In contrast to many books I have written, this project presented a unique challenge because of the sheer volume of resources available: the proverbial problem of "taking a sip of water from an open fire hose." There is a wealth of published material, including an extensive array of unit histories, technical histories of the various bombers and fighter types, and many general histories of strategic bombing from a variety of perspectives. My attempt here was to step back and try to present a broader picture of the forest rather than take a detailed look at the trees.

There are several excellent accounts of Operation *Pointblank* from the American and German perspectives, with the McFarland and Newton account being a noteworthy example from the American perspective and the Caldwell and Muller book from the Luftwaffe's perspective. Boog's official history from the Militärgeschichtliches Forschungsamt (Military History Research Institute) in Potsdam is also noteworthy, but is apt to be less known to Osprey readers because of the prohibitive cost of the English-language edition. While most accounts of the Luftwaffe focus on the fighters, the Golücke book on the Schweinfurt battle provides an exceptionally well-rounded account of German defense efforts with extensive detail on flak and command-and-control. The Svejgaard book, while focused on Denmark, provides one of the few detailed English accounts on the evolution of Luftwaffe command-and-control. The bibliography listed below is only a fraction of the volumes that I used to prepare this book.

Besides the massive amount of published material, there are extensive archival resources. Some of these are particularly worth mentioning since they are available as downloads from the Internet such as those at the US Air Force Historical Research Center site. This site has all of the official US Air Force historical studies that were prepared immediately after the war. Although not as well known as the US Army's Foreign Military Studies series, the US Air Force historical center prepared a parallel series of Luftwaffe histories under the direction of General der Flieger Paul Deichmann and Generalleutnant Hermann Plocher, which were included in the series. Several of those relating to Reich defense are listed below.

The workhorse of the early escort fighters was the P-47 Thunderbolt. This is a P-47D-11-RE "razorback" prior to the introduction of the D-15 version, which introduced wing pylons to carry drop tanks. This particular aircraft flew with the 374th Fighter Squadron, 361st Fighter Group, from RAF Bottisham and was photographed here while flying very close to a B-17. (NARA)

While the US Strategic Bombing Survey is well known, particularly the published volume on the aircraft industry, what are not as well known are the extensive array of unpublished technical memos prepared in support of the main reports. So for example in the case of Report No. 59 on "The Defeat of the Luftwaffe," there are several detailed studies on "German Air Force Order of Battles and Losses;" "German Air Force Planning and Requirements in Relation to Production," "The Impact of the Allied Air Effort on the German Air Force Program for Training Day Fighter Pilots," and "The German Flak Effort Throughout the War," as well as supporting interviews with key German officials. These records are contained within the US Strategic Bombing Survey files at the US National Archives and Records Administration at College Park, Maryland, in Record Group 243.

US Strategic Bombing Survey reports
The Effects of Strategic Bombing on the German War Economy (No. 3, Office of the Chairman)
Aircraft Division Industry Report (No. 4, Aircraft Division)
The Defeat of the German Air Force (No. 59, Military Analysis Division)

US Air Force historical studies
Boylan, Bernard, *Development of the Long-Range Escort Fighter* (No. 136, 1955)
Ferguson, Arthur, *The Early Operations of the Eighth Air Force and the Origins of the Combined Bomber Offensive, 17 August 1942 to 10 June 1943* (No. 118, 1946)
Grabmann, Walter, *German Air Force Air Defense Operations* (No. 164, 1956)
Heinrichs, Waldo, *A History of the VIII USAAF Fighter Command* (n.d.)
Kammhuber, Josef, *Problems in the Conduct of a Day and Night Defensive Air War* (No. 179, 1953)
Nielsen, Andreas L. and Grabmann, Walter, *Anglo-American Techniques of Strategic Warfare in the Air* (No. 183, 1957)
Norris, Joe, *The Combined Bomber Offensive: 1 January to 6 June 1944* (No. 122, 1947)
Ramsey, John, *The War Against the Luftwaffe: USAAF Counter-Air Operations April 1943–June 1944* (No. 110, 1945)
Renz, Otto von, *The Development of German Antiaircraft Weapons and Equipment of All Types up to 1945* (No. 194, 1958)
Schmid, Josef, *The German Air Force versus the Allies in the West: German Air Defense* (No. 159, 1954)
Schmid, Josef and Grabmann, Walter, *The German Air Force versus the Allies in the West: The Air War in the West* (No. 158, 1954)
Suchenwirth, Richard, *Command and Leadership in the German Air Force* (No. 174, 1969)
Stormont, John, *The Combined Bomber Offensive, April thru December 1943* (No. 119, 1946)

Books
Boog, Horst, et al., *Germany and the Second World War, Vol VII: The Strategic Air War in Europe* (Oxford: 2006)
Caldwell, Donald and Muller, Richard, *The Luftwaffe over Germany: Defense of the Reich* (Greenhill: 2007)

Cox, Sebastian (ed.), *The Strategic Air War against Germany 1939–45* (Frank Cass: 1998)

Craven, W. F. and Cate, J. L., *The Army Air Forces in World War II, Vol. 2 – Europe: TORCH to POINTBLANK* (University of Chicago: 1951)

——, *The Army Air Forces in World War II, Vol. 3 – Europe: ARGUMENT to VE Day* (University of Chicago: 1951)

Davis, Richard, *Carl Spaatz and the Air War in Europe* (Center for Air Force History: 1983)

Jong, Ivo de, *Mission 376: Battle over the Reich 28 May 1944* (Hikoki: 2003)

Dewez, Luc and Faley, Michale, *High Noon over Haseluenne: The 100th Bombardment Group over Berlin, March 6, 1944* (Schiffer: 2009)

Ehlers, Robert, *Targeting the Third Reich: Allied Intelligence and the Allied Bombing Campaigns* (University Press of Kansas: 2009)

Ethell, Jeffrey and Price, Alfred, *Target Berlin: Mission 250: 6 March 1944* (Arms & Armour: 1989)

Freeman, Roger, *The Mighty Eighth: A History of the US 8th Army Air Force* (Doubleday: 1970)

——, *The Mighty Eighth War Diary* (Arms & Armour: 1981)

——, *The Mighty Eighth War Manual* (Arms & Armour: 1984)

Golücke, Friedhelm, *Schweinfurt und der strategische Luftkrieg 1943* (Schoningh: 1980)

Hansen, Randall, *Fire and Fury: The Allied Bombing of Germany 1942–1945* (Penguin: 2009)

Irving, David, *The Rise and Fall of the Luftwaffe: The Life of Field Marshal Erhard Milch* (Little, Brown: 1973)

Isby, David (ed.), *Fighting the Bombers: The Luftwaffe's Struggle against the Allied Bomber Offensive* (Greenhill: 2003)

Kuylen, Jaap van der, *The Killing Sky: Black Tuesday 11 January 1944* (Rijpsma: 2004)

Ludwig, Paul, *Development of the P-51 Mustang Long-Range Escort Fighter* (Classic: 2003)

McFarland, Stephen and Newton, Wesley, *To Command the Sky: The Battle for Air Superiority over Germany 1942–44* (Smithsonian: 1991)

Price, Alfred, *Battle over the Reich* (Ian Allen: 1973)

——, *Battle over the Reich: The Strategic Bomber Offensive over Germany, Volume Two 1943–45* (Ian Allen: 2005)

Murray, Williamson, *Strategy for Defeat: The Luftwaffe 1933–45* (Air University Press: 1983)

Svejgaard, M., *Der Luftnachrichten Dienst in Denmark* (Gyges: 2003)

Westermann, Edward, *Flak: German Anti-Aircraft Defenses 1914–45* (University Press of Kansas: 2001)

INDEX

References to illustrations are shown in **bold**.
Plates are shown with page in **bold** and caption
in brackets, e.g. **4** (5).